FANTASIES CAN COME TRUE.
THEY CAN HAPPEN TO YOU.

"The guard is going to punish his prisoner," Dave murmured, "and there's nothing she can do about it." As he watched Judy's face, he realized he was as excited as she was by the images on the movie screen. Yes, he wanted to see his wife tied up, at his mercy, and it was clear she wanted it, too. Dave vowed to make it happen . . .

Cory's massages were always professional. His face was immobile while he stroked and kneaded the firm flesh of his female clients, never letting his hands move in an erotic manner. Until he met Lilia . . .

At midnight, the guests unmasked and their host announced the prize winners. To no one's surprise, Susan, dressed as a sexy girl pirate, and Frank, her half-naked slave and bodyguard, won first prize. But the best prize for both of them came a little later, once they got home . . .

"I could make you a crystal that would make you irresistible to men," said the wizard to the love-lorn Gabrielle, "but you would have to agree to my conditions. I just want to watch you and some handsome man make love right here in my workroom."

"Is that really all?" the beautiful Gabrielle replied . . .

Joan Lloyd is a high school teacher who lives outside of New York City. Of herself, she says, "Like 'J,' the author of *The Sensuous Woman,* I'm someone who stumbled on new activities to increase the range of my sexual activity. And I've found a new way to communicate with my sexual partner—a way that works. I wrote this book to share with you the wonderful things I've learned."

Nice COUPLES *Do*

How to Turn Your Secret Dreams into Sensational Sex.

Joan Elizabeth Lloyd

WARNER BOOKS

A Time Warner Company

Warner Books, Inc., 1271 Avenue of the Americas, New York, NY 10020

 A Time Warner Company

Printed in the United States of America
First printing: August 1991
10 9 8 7 6

Library of Congress Cataloging-in-Publication Data

Lloyd, Joan Elizabeth.
  Nice couples do : how to turn your secret dreams into
sensational sex / Joan Elizabeth Lloyd.
    p. cm.
  ISBN 0-446-39258-8
    1. Sex instruction.   2. Sexual fantasies.   I. Title.
HQ31.L66   1991
613.9′6—dc20   91-8249
                                                      CIP

Cover photo by Hermann Estevez

Cover design by Anne Twomey

Book design by Giorgetta Bell McRee

This book is dedicated:
To my family, immediate and extended,
*   for all their support.*
To Jamie and Meg for all their help.
To 'Pete' for showing me how.
To Ed for teaching me why.

If you are the recipient of this book, don't panic.
Someone is trying to tell you something wonderful.

CONTENTS

1   MY STORY   1

2   BOOKMARKING—WHY AND HOW   13

3   UNSPOKEN CLUES   29

4   FIRST TIMES   59

5   EROTIC SURROUNDINGS   79

6   GAMES OF CONTROL   85

7   TOYS   111

8   MASSAGE   121

9   DIRTY TALK   128

10   ANAL SEX   136

11   AVOIDING SOME PITFALLS   146

12   BEDTIME STORIES   156

13   STORY STARTERS   202

CONCLUSION   227

1

MY STORY

Ten years ago, my husband and I divorced after almost twenty years of marriage. The reasons are irrelevant. My marriage had been over for a long time before my husband and I actually separated. After my husband departed, I felt great relief and I'm sure he felt the same. We went our separate ways without much rancor and are still friends.

Typical children of our generation, when we married in the early sixties we were just out of our teens. My husband had some sexual experience, gained in the front seat of his car. I had none. Therefore, we had no way of knowing what was possible or what we enjoyed.

So we explored. We petted in his 1956 Chevy while listening to rock music and watching the "submarine races." I can still remember how my hunger was satisfied when he touched my breasts. I had never gone further so his touching my nipples was a culmination of some kind.

Then, when he first touched my vagina, through my underpants, again there was a degree of satisfaction. This continued through his touching my bare skin, putting his fingers inside me, and my learning the rudiments of touching him. Each time we took a step forward into a land where I had never been before, it was exhilarating.

The first time we made love—yes, it was making love and not just fucking—it was delicious. I couldn't get enough of the feeling of him inside of me. It was missionary position, but that was fine with me.

Through my years of marriage, I read. As romance novels became popular, I read books by Rosemary Rogers, Jennifer Wilde, and Danielle Steele. In some, there were actual descriptions of sex; in others, the author just alluded to it. Always, the sexual exploits of the hero and heroine were of a type that I had never experienced. I thought they were only the stuff of fiction.

I started to think that maybe there was more to sex than missionary position quickies or missionary position longies, but I had no idea how to talk to my husband about sex.

Understand that I'm not faulting my husband. It was mutual ignorance. I didn't know what I wanted, and even if I had, I wouldn't have known how to ask for it. He may well have had the same problem.

At thirty, I learned about masturbation and practiced until I could give myself a physically satisfying orgasm. I frequently did so in the bathroom in the middle of the night, after a particularly erotic dream or a less-than-fulfilling experience with my husband.

In the late seventies, after my divorce, I began the sexual experimentation that I hadn't done as a young adult. I quickly learned that one-night stands weren't sexually rewarding. On the contrary, they usually left me more frustrated than I had been when I started. They were good for my ego, since I repeatedly proved to myself that I was an attractive woman, but they did not satisfy my desire to make something more out of my sex life.

In 1983, a small incident with a man in my office introduced me to the world of creative sex and provided me with the key to my own ability to communicate sexually.

I had been having lunch with a man, whom I will call Pete, once a week for a few months. Our talks had gotten intimate enough so that he knew I was unattached and hungry. He was certainly hitting on me and I was willing to be hit upon.

He was also recently divorced and a bit more uninhibited in his conversation than I was. Gradually, he revealed that he was involved in a few sexual relationships, one of which involved sexual activities that were, shall we say, not in the mainstream.

Although I blushed as he described some of these activities, I think my face quickly revealed that I was titillated. He asked me whether I had ever considered "spicing up my sex life." I didn't know exactly how to respond. I couldn't admit anything, so I stammered some inane reply. He sensed my communication problem.

"It has always upset me," he said, "that two people could be interested in the same thing and never have the ability to communicate what that is."

"Yeah, me, too," was all that I could say.

"Maybe I have a way that we can explore our mutual interests without talking."

I was fascinated, but Pete changed the subject and we parted that afternoon without my learning anything more.

The next morning, I found a copy of an erotic magazine in a paper bag on my desk chair. There was a note attached.

> Read this magazine sometime when you're alone. Find an article that excites you. Put a bookmark in the appropriate page and put the magazine in my top desk drawer.

The note was signed P.

I had never read a magazine like this one, which specialized in exotic sex. There was a section on voyeurism, one on threesomes, and one, which nearly drove me crazy, on bondage.

Three days later, I crept into Pete's office before he arrived at work and, with trembling hands, I put the magazine in his desk. I had put a bookmark in an article about a woman who had been tied to a bed, teased, and eventually well fucked.

NICE COUPLES DO   5

Just before lunch, Pete stuck his head into my office. I was on a long-distance phone call, so I couldn't talk to him. I didn't have to. He walked over to my chair and tied a thin ribbon around my wrist. Then, surreptitiously, he stroked the obvious bulge in the front of his slacks. Then he winked and left.

I could hardly sit still. I completed my phone call and, with my heart pounding, I went into his office.

"Is that really what interests you?" Pete asked without preamble.

I still couldn't talk about it. I just nodded.

"Would you like me to tie you up like the woman in the article and make love to you for hours?" he asked.

I couldn't have said a word. I swallowed hard and just nodded again.

"How about after work today, my place. I'll meet you by the elevators at five-thirty. And just leave the ribbon around your wrist to remind you of what we're going to do later." As if I could forget.

The rest of my brief relationship with Pete is history. Let me just say that our time together was a turning point in my sex life.

I spent the next few years trying to communicate my desires for unconventional sex with my partners. A few were unreceptive and thought that sexual creativity was something for whores and their johns. Nice girls weren't interested in those things, or shouldn't be. I tried to explain that enjoyment is where you find it and that there are all kinds of experiences in the world, but their minds were closed. Those relationships didn't last long.

Other men were freer than I had been and were able to communicate desires of all types. We talked and played and enjoyed.

With still others, introducing the topic of varied sex and establishing a dialogue opened a world of sexual experimentation. Once or twice, what a man suggested was not my cup of tea. I merely said, in one way or another, "How about this instead." Sometimes, he wasn't interested in an activity I mentioned. One of us then suggested something else. Never did we fail to find something mutually exciting and rewarding.

During those years of exploration, I came to some conclusions. I believe that most of us have desires that go unexpressed and therefore unfulfilled. Some men go to prostitutes to do the things of which they are sure their wives would disapprove. Both men and women use singles bars to pick up partners for an evening of dinner and bed, hoping that variety will indeed be the spice of their lives.

However, while we used to be able to freely go outside of our primary relationship to try to find what we'd been looking for, it is now imperative for us to find a way to communicate our desires to our partner and try new activities at home. In the age of AIDS, sport fucking is a thing of the past, or soon will be. The penalty for promiscuity may be death. We must do our experimenting at home! And that is where the fun begins.

For the last five years, I have had a monogamous relationship with a wonderful man named Ed. Over those years, Ed and I have discovered and explored our varied appetites, and they are, in most cases, not very different. We more than meet each other's needs and we still experiment and find new things to enjoy together. That is not to say that all our experiments give both of us equal pleasure. Some games we have tried and discarded because one or the other of us didn't enjoy them.

What is the secret of our mutual exploration? First, we have accepted that anything we want to try that doesn't hurt anyone and that gives us both pleasure is okay. Second, we have learned how to communicate—how to make suggestions and how to say no. Third, we have learned that a fully rewarding sexual life is worth the limited risks we do take and we have learned how to communicate to minimize those risks. We have explored many areas of off-center sex, using bookmarking, as Pete and I did. We expanded by using erotic stories both to excite each other and to explore other sexual possibilities. We had to learn through experience, and we made many mistakes along the way.

Over the years since Pete and I first explored new types of sexual activity, I have read many books about creative sex. I looked for suggestions about other activities Ed and I could try and some of the problems we might encounter with them. I had hoped that some would help me to avoid various awkward situations my partner and I got into. While many of those other books and articles said "Try something new," "Make love in the bathroom," "Buy some sexy lingerie or some sex toys," none of them went into much detail about what to try or how to get past the embarrassment of trying to buy toys or underwear. None of them talked about rug burns or giggling at just the wrong moment or why I don't have seventeen orgasms every night. And none of them covered ways to minimize the risks while you communicate a desire to be tied to the bed or to try anal sex. My partner and I had to muddle through on our own and we learned a lot.

So now you know about me. Like J, the author of *The Sensuous Woman,* I'm someone who stumbled on new ways to increase the range of my sexual activity. And I've found a new way to communicate with my sexual partner—a way that works. I wrote this book to share with you the wonderful things I've learned.

This book goes further than any other book you've read about sexual creativity. It will use both narrative and erotic literature to suggest new activities that might be enjoyable both to you and your partner. It will also discuss some communication techniques that I have used to suggest things about which I had a hard time talking. It will cover many of the things that I have learned the hard way so you can avoid some of the awkwardness and embarrassment I've experienced.

As you read, try to keep your mind open. You

needn't be interested in "kinky sex" to benefit. This book can help you express any desires from "I think I'd like to be touched this way" to "Have you ever considered making love while dangling from a chandelier?"

Nothing I will say here is a panacea, a cure-all for an ailing relationship. In any relationship, however, there are new things that remain to be discovered if partners can find a way to communicate. Wouldn't it be a shame if you and your partner had the same sexual fantasies but you never found a way to share them?

So the intention of this book is to assist communication, not to advocate a change in your lifestyle—unless you want one.

WRITING THIS BOOK

Pronouns were a problem for me as I wrote this book. As a woman, I tend to write from the female point of view. However, there is very little here that is specific to one sex or the other. So I often use the word *partner,* trying to avoid references to the gender of your vis-à-vis.

Personally, I am irritated by attempts to eliminate sexism in books by using a he/she construction. It offends my ear, if nothing else, and much of this book is meant to be read aloud. However, in writing this book, it was sometimes necessary to use the words *he* or *she.* I solved the problem in the only way I felt I could. I used the words at random, sometimes changing the gender in the middle of a paragraph. In most cases, the gender of the character is immaterial. Of course, if you are reading aloud, change the pronouns to suit.

There may be women reading this who feel that there are situations and suggestions that are anti-feminist or chauvinistic, that the man's needs dominate my writing. I'm not advocating turning any woman into a sex machine whose job it is to please her man at the expense of her self. As a matter of fact, I'm saying just the opposite. Both sexes have needs, valid ones that deserve to be discussed and satisfied, as long as both partners agree. Being sexy is in no way antifeminist. One of the goals of the feminist movement is to make women aware of their own needs and desires and convince them to ask for what they want. Relax and don't get hung up on sexism.

Besides sexism, words presented me with another problem in writing this book. I read a lot of erotic literature and I am sometimes turned off by what I read. Most of the time, my reactions are triggered not by the actions involved but by the language used. Therefore, one of the hardest decisions I've had to make while writing this book was what to call vaginas and penises.

One approach is to call genitals by their correct anatomical names. However, some people find those terms very clinical and a sexual turnoff. I sympathize. A colorful phrase here and there titillates the senses and adds to erotic stimulation.

On the other hand, many erotic magazines go to extraordinary lengths to use "sexy" words and phrases and to avoid repetition. Personally, I find the terms *hungry love tunnel* and *throbbing pole* turnoffs. Those publishers sell magazines, though, so there must be people out there who find those phrases exciting.

The end result of all my editorial musing was the rerealization that what turns some people on, turns others off, and, of course, that's what this book is about.

Therefore, in writing this book, I have used the words *penis* and *vagina,* as well as *cock, cunt,* and *pussy.* I think they are terms that will not offend too many readers.

As you already know, the book you are reading is about sex. It is explicit, filled with erotic stories and suggestions that you can use to enhance your sexual relationship.

If you usually skip the sexy parts of a novel because you want to get on with the story, or you won't see an R-rated movie for fear of being grossed out, maybe you shouldn't continue reading. Put the book back on the shelf or, if you have already bought it, give it to a friend who might benefit from it.

If you have received this book as a gift from a husband, wife, or lover, congratulations. Someone out there is trying to tell you something wonderful—to suggest that there are new things that you might enjoy together.

If there are sections that you view as "kinky," and they offend you, skip them.

Most important, don't prejudge. If you find yourself labeling the book as a whole or sections of it "good" or "bad," stop. Suspend your value judgments. Things that are enjoyed privately by you and your partner harm no one and can improve your relationship. And the communication skills that you master in the bedroom cannot help but spill over into other aspects of your life together.

Remember, the only important value judgments are "I never considered that before, but it might feel good," or "That doesn't sound like something I would enjoy," or even "Yuch. Not my thing."

Now that you know why I wrote this book and how I wrote it, settle back and open your mind. Read and enjoy.

2

BOOKMARKING—
WHY AND HOW

Bookmarking, the technique that Pete and I used to explore our mutual interests, worked well for us. Throughout this book, I have used stories to illustrate my ideas and I'm suggesting that you use the same stories to communicate with your partner.

Why do we need help discussing sex with our partner? Because many of us have never learned how. As a matter of fact, many of us never learned that it was okay or even possible to admit to ourselves that we wanted or needed something different, much less to discuss those needs with anyone.

Sexual communication in its simplest form has been going on since the first caveman grunted his version of "Assume the position," and the first cavewoman grunted back, "Not tonight, dear, I have a headache."

Over the years, mankind has come a long way. Books such as *The Joy of Sex* and *Everything You*

Always Wanted to Know About Sex . . . have taught us much. Dr. Ruth Westheimer has done a herculean job of dragging us, stammering and blushing, out of the dark ages of sexual communication. We now read articles such as "How to Achieve Orgasm in Your Camper," "Fun with Ice and Feathers," and "The Erogenous Zone that Brings Instant Orgasm" in our favorite magazines. Most of us can now even say *vagina* and *penis* without giggling.

Some of us have come far enough to say to our partner, "I'd like to try something different," but can we verbalize what that something is? I'm afraid many of us can't.

Maybe she would like to tell him that she would like to play doctor. Maybe he would like to tell her that he would enjoy being spanked.

But sexual communication carries risk.

Will he think that he's not satisfying me and will he be terribly hurt?

Will she think I'm not man enough to become aroused by what we're already doing?

Will he think that I'm some kind of pervert for wanting something that's a little off center?

Will she be so turned off by my suggestion that she'll never get excited by me again?

Will he think that I'm not woman enough to be excited by the ordinary?

Will she laugh at me?

Will he think I'm a bimbo?

Will she be mad?

Will he be mad? And on and on . . .

The rewards of successful sexual communication are enormous. I think that most people want to please both their partner and themselves, and throughout this book I'll try to help you discover ways to do both.

Before we explore what to try, let me try to answer one basic question. How can you minimize the risk? I am advocating nonspoken, nonthreatening sexual communication. That's part of what this book is about: using erotic literature as a tool.

Erotic writing and storytelling is designed to arouse and stimulate lovemaking. The word *erotica* comes from the Greek *erotikos,* "of or caused by love." That Greek word derives from Eros, the Greek god of love. Please don't confuse this with pornography, which is defined as "written, graphic, or other forms of communication intended to excite lascivious [lustful or lewd] feelings." This word comes from *porne,* the Greek word for harlot.

I'm suggesting that you use erotica as a communication tool the way I did with Pete and still do with Ed.

There are two ways to start. Either read this book yourself, then use a bookmark to indicate something that excites you, and give the volume to your partner to read in private, or give the book to your partner unmarked and let him or her do the bookmarking.

Of course, if, while you're reading, you find a section of this book so exciting that you want to put the book aside and make passionate love to your partner, forget the bookmark and go for it. If you're lucky, it will take weeks for you to finish the book and you'll enjoy the frequent interludes even before you start bookmarking.

Don't feel that you have to read all the stories I've written. Some may not interest you. However, by reading the entire book, you may become aware of sexual games that you never thought about before but that intrigue you. There are also small items in each story that you might want to mark: a particular position or a place to make love, a toy to play with, or a role to play.

After you have read as much as you want, select an idea, a situation, a position, or whatever and mark it. Use a bookmark, dog-ear the page, or underline or highlight a particular sentence or paragraph. Then give this book to your partner, or leave it where he can find it. If you want to, you can read sections of the book aloud.

Another way to use this volume is to give the unmarked book to your partner and suggest that he bookmark a section and give it back to you. But whatever way you choose to use this book, continue to use it. Your first bookmark shouldn't be your last.

Don't panic if you are the recipient of the book, unmarked. Open your mind and relax. Someone is trying to tell you something wonderful. You have just gotten one of the best compliments you have ever received. Your partner has said to you, "I think that you are open-minded enough to understand what I am trying to tell you. I want to have fun with you. I want us to enjoy something new, together. I don't want to fantasize alone anymore. I want to share my fantasies with you or even act one out. What would you like to try?"

Do what I did. Select a story that appeals to you and put a bookmark on the first page of the article. If only a small section of a story appeals to you, mark the page, or write in the margin.

If the idea of acting out a situation or trying a new scenario doesn't appeal to you yet, bookmark one of the "Bedtime Stories" at the end of the book that might be fun to read aloud or just read silently together. Be sure to clarify whether you want to read aloud or act out.

Whatever you've chosen, give the book back to your partner. If you find the whole thing very embarrassing, that's all right. Slip the book under your partner's pillow, on the seat of the car, or in a briefcase.

Notice that it is not necessary to speak, or even to face each other. Your embarrassment needn't be obvious. You can pretend to be as suave as you like, although it's probably unnecessary. Most likely your partner will be as nervous as you are.

Now relax and wait to see what happens.

What should you do if you are the recipient of a bookmarked article?

Smile. Your partner has just said something wonderful to you. She has just said, "Here is a secret that I haven't shared with anyone. It's a delicious idea that might appeal to you and might enhance our sexual and sensual time together. I want to share this idea. Does it appeal to you?"

There are, of course, two answers to that unspoken question.

If the idea doesn't appeal to you, read the book yourself and move the bookmark. Slip a note in the newly selected page and say, "How about this instead?" The book can pass back and forth until you find a mutually satisfying selection. Maybe you'll find only a small passage. That's all right, too. You've just opened a sexual dialogue, without words. Other forms of communication will grow from it.

It is most important that your body language reinforce your desire to continue to communicate in order to find a mutual pleasure. This is a very delicate moment and your partner has taken a risk. He has risked your disapproval. Tread very gently. If his idea of something wonderful is about as far from yours as it can get, that's okay. Just don't convey the feeling that there is something "bad" about what was just communicated. Remember one of the premises upon which this book is based: Nothing that two people enjoy doing together is "bad." People's ideas of what's sexually stimulating are often different.

If the idea that your partner has suggested appeals to you, that's wonderful. Very often, two people have had the same fantasies for a long time but never knew it.

Now you have to figure out how to bring your

mutual desires from fantasy to reality. What a wonderful problem.

First, get rid of the kids. Send them to their grandparents. Swap them out with a neighbor. Hire a baby-sitter and rent a motel room for the evening. Put a lock on your bedroom door, if necessary.

Then, set the scene, if that's appropriate. Have a good dinner. Put soft music on the stereo. Have some wine. Anticipation is a large part of the fun, but it's also a nervous time. Each of you is looking for any hint of disapproval from the other, so you must each continually and deliberately send positive messages. Smile. Touch. Kiss. Whisper. Take a warm shower—together.

Then, while in the throes of your new experience, continue to send positive messages. "That feels so good." "I love it when you do that." "Move over this way so I can enjoy you more." Purr, groan, make the sounds that your partner has come to understand as positive feedback. Don't expect your partner to guess. Tell him or her before, during, and after.

If you're acting out a scene, get into it. Use the appropriate tone of voice, be young, old, masterful, subservient, hesitant, knowledgeable, ignorant, whatever is called for. And if you find you have the urge to giggle, do so. I was always afraid that my laughter would send the wrong message and ruin the mood. When a chuckle slipped out, I apologized. I was amazed how often laughing was my partner's urge at that moment, too, and he was just as afraid about killing the mood. Don't worry. A good laugh during sex is a great positive reinforcer. It also reduces the level of sexual tension a bit, so you can increase it again. And that's an unexpected bonus that prolongs your lovemaking.

There is one more important thing—your reaction afterward. The question that will be on your partner's mind, as well as yours, is "Was it really okay?" Each time you take a new step, you need to know and to communicate to your partner that it's really okay. I still tell my partner that whatever new experience we just tried was okay and I still need to be told, as well. And don't confuse okay with enjoyable. Okay means that you are not repelled by the fact that your partner tried something different. Even if you didn't enjoy what you just did, be sure he understands that it was all right for him to try new things. It was the activity, not him, that you didn't enjoy.

It's possible that although an activity seemed all right while you were very excited, later, in the cold light of morning, you realize that it wasn't something that you are anxious to repeat. Or maybe you were willing to give it a try since your partner seemed so interested but it didn't work out for you. Talk this over, too. Be honest, and suggest an alternative for the future.

I spoke about minimizing risk. When you and your partner have tried something different, you must reinforce the reward. You can say, "That was wonderful—I enjoyed it," or you can just purr. Don't forget to send those nonverbal signals, too.

Touch and cuddle to ease doubts, both yours and your partner's.

Alice and Tony's story illustrates how one couple might have used this book to explore a new sexual activity that Tony hadn't known how to discuss with his wife.

ALICE AND TONY'S STORY

It was pouring when Alice returned from waiting for the school bus with her three children. She shed her raincoat, put her open umbrella in the down-stairs bathtub, and poured herself a much-needed cup of coffee. Cup in hand, she slowly climbed the stairs to make the beds, clean the bathroom, and tidy up after the children and her husband, Tony.

With a sigh, she walked into the bedroom and set her coffee mug on her bedside table. Then she noticed the book. It was lying on her pillow, with a bookmark on top and a note saying simply, "I Love You." She picked up the note and looked at the book beneath. The cover was unmistakable. It was that book about kinky sex.

Heavily, she sat down on the bed and her hands began to shake. She knew all about the book but had never actually seen a copy.

Why was Tony giving her a sex manual? After all,

that was what it was. What was Tony trying to tell her? Was he upset with her? Was there another woman?

She squared her shoulders. Don't get yourself all worked up, she told herself. You're overreacting. She looked at the note still in her hand. "I Love You."

Tony must be telling me that he wants to spice up our sex life. She was amazed. She had thought that it was only she who was dissatisfied with their sex life. She set the note and the book down on the bureau and walked over to the full-length mirror on the back of the bedroom door. She studied her reflection.

Her hair was brown and curly and tended to frizz a bit when it was damp, as it was now. Her hazel eyes were surrounded by long lashes. She looked better with eye makeup, but she usually didn't bother to use it except when she and Tony were going out.

Her nose was small, as was her mouth. Hers was not an exciting face, but not a dreadful one, either. Alice pulled at the back of her oversized sweater, stretching it tightly across her small breasts and flat stomach. For a woman of forty, she thought, I haven't got a bad figure at all.

She walked back over to the bureau and looked down at the book—a sex manual.

Tony and Alice had been married for fourteen years and their sex life wasn't very exciting any-more, but it was usually pleasant. Alice had read articles in the magazines she got at the supermarket about how to jazz up your sex life, and she occasionally considered actually doing something. But on the rare occasion that she had thought about something creative, she realized anew that she hadn't a clue how to talk to Tony about such topics. So she had learned to be content, only rarely acknowledging her vague feeling that there could be more to her bedroom relationship with her husband.

With a sigh, Alice left the book on the bureau and spent the next hour tidying the house. After finishing the bathrooms, she wandered back into her bedroom.

As she pulled the sheets tight and stretched the bedspread across the blankets, her eyes strayed to the book still resting on the bureau. She threw Tony's dirty underwear into the hamper and glanced at her bedside clock: 11:15. Still lots of time before lunch.

Slowly, she walked over and picked the book up. She sat down on the edge of the bed, turned to the first page, and started reading. By the time she reached page seven, she had made herself more comfortable and stretched her legs out on the bedspread. It took a half hour for her to finish the first chapter. Already, she had blushed and giggled out loud at some of the things she had read, but she was still reading.

"Someone is trying to tell you something wonderful." The words from the book kept echoing in her head as she read. Tony is trying to tell me something nice. She turned to the next chapter and kept reading. Some of the activities discussed sounded so outrageous to her that she skipped whole pages. Occasionally, she looked around guiltily, as though someone might catch her enjoying other sections.

She heard the front door slam and glanced at the clock: 3:30. Where had the day gone? She hadn't finished the book, but she knew that she would read the rest another time. And one story in particular had given her chills. Did she dare to do what the book suggested and bookmark that story before giving the book back to Tony?

She slammed the book shut, slid it under her bed, and went downstairs. All afternoon, despite two trips to after-school activities and one to the supermarket, that one story hadn't left her mind.

Could she? Did Tony really mean that she should use the bookmark he had left for her? Did she really want Tony to know what she was thinking? Would he be shocked or angry? Oh God, she thought, what should I do?

"Someone is trying to tell you something wonderful." Over and over, that message echoed in her head. Tony wants to try new things. He must really want to know what I want or he wouldn't have given me the book in the first place.

As Alice stirred a pot of spaghetti sauce, she made up her mind. She dashed upstairs and retrieved the book from under her bed. Before she could change her mind, she found the section she wanted and put the bookmark in it. Then she put

NICE COUPLES DO 25

the book on Tony's bed table and half-buried it under some magazines.

Without looking back, she scurried downstairs.

Tony had spent the day at work unable to concentrate. Why had he left that book for Alice? he wondered for the umpteenth time. But he knew why.

It had all started two weeks earlier in the steam room at his health club. He had just finished a particularly hard game of racquetball and was enjoying the heat and a few moments of relaxation.

As he sat, he tuned in to a conversation that two men across the room were having. It was so steamy that he couldn't see them clearly, but he could hear every word.

"She really went down on you?" one man was saying.

"She not only sucked my cock but she seemed to enjoy it," the second man said. "I've wanted her to do that for as long as I can remember. And that book was the start of it all."

Tony was fascinated. He had always wanted Alice to touch him and put her mouth on his penis. He had never dared ask because he was sure that she would be shocked and repelled. A few times, she had touched him during their lovemaking, and each time he tried to tell her how wonderful her hands felt, but the words wouldn't come out. He had hoped his exaggerated body language would show her what he wanted, but, unfortunately, his message had never gotten through to Alice and the touching was not often repeated.

"She really wasn't turned off when you gave her the book?" the first man was saying.

"Not at all. She read it all but paid particular attention to the section I had bookmarked." Tony could almost hear the man's grin. "The rest is history. She's going to mark a section for me next."

"*Nice Couples Do . . .* ," the second man said. "I wonder whether I could give a copy to Jeanmarie?"

Tony had heard about the book. If it would only work, he thought.

It had taken two days for Tony to get up the nerve to buy a copy and three more before he finally had opened it and started reading. He had had his lunch in his office for the next few days while he read and debated with himself.

He had wanted to mark a section for her, one on touching, but he hadn't been brave enough. She won't be as negative if I give the book to her and let her select something, he had reasoned. Will she understand? I don't want to louse up what I have, but I know we could have so much more. That morning, he had gathered his courage and placed the volume, with the bookmark and the note, on her pillow.

Tony had been jumpy as a nervous bride all day and had put off leaving the office until he ran out of work on his desk. Hesitantly, he got his raincoat and slowly made his way home. During the trip, he agonized. He could tell her it all had been a mistake. He hadn't understood about the book. A guy in his office thought she might enjoy it. He could make up some excuse and take the book back.

He walked into the house, ready to offer some explanation, but when he saw Alice standing in the kitchen making dinner, he knew he had done the right thing, whatever the outcome. I love her so much, he thought. I want to recapture some of that wonderful newness we had when we were first married.

It was obvious from the strained tone in her voice when she said hello that Alice had found the book, but Tony couldn't gauge her reaction, not with all the children regaling them with tales of their day at school. There is still time to bail out, he thought. No! I'm going to see it through.

During dinner, neither Tony nor Alice said much. Each of the three children had a long, involved problem that had to be discussed. It was lucky that they didn't have to make conversation. They were both too nervous.

As the children started to clear the dishes, Tony asked, "Did you see the book I left you?" His voice was barely audible and Alice had to strain to hear him.

She nodded. "I read it," she said. She stood up and picked up the empty spaghetti bowl. Her hands were shaking so hard that she almost dropped it. "It's on your bed table."

As Alice watched, Tony fumbled with his napkin, pushed his chair back noisily, and hurried upstairs. He's as anxious and nervous as I am, she thought. I wonder whether he's as excited.

Alice finished the dishes and left the children in front of the TV. Slowly, she walked upstairs. Tony was stretched out on his side of the bed, his long legs crossed at the ankles. His straight dark brown hair was slightly mussed and his glasses sat on the end of his nose as he read. Alice smiled. He's really a very sexy man, she thought. Her eyes strayed to the obvious bulge in the front of his slacks.

"You understood what I meant?" he asked as he heard Alice come in.

"Eventually. It frightened me at first, but after I did some reading, I understood. You were trying to tell me something wonderful."

Tony grinned. "I love you very much, but there's so much I can't talk about."

"Me, too."

"Really? You marked this section?" he asked, holding up the bookmark.

"Yes," she answered shyly.

"You really mean it?"

Alice smiled and there was a glint in her eye. Tony had his answer.

Alice and Tony's story concerns two people who wanted more from their sex life, two people who now have taken the first step. They have opened a dialogue and found a comfortable way to discuss methods to spice up their monogamous relationship. There are, of course, other ways to find out about each other's desires.

3

UNSPOKEN CLUES

It is certainly possible to discover your mutual likes and dislikes without talking about them directly. Those discoveries are usually made by accident, though, not by design. It's possible to try new things when you don't even know what those things are. Ed and I are proof that mistakes don't ruin a relationship.

There are many times when your partner gives you an unspoken clue, some indication that he wants something different or that he's particularly enjoying some activity. Don't overlook these. They are valuable on their own and in combination with other ways to share ideas.

If Maggie hadn't correctly interpreted Larry's reading habits, she might never have found the way to enhance their sexual life together.

MAGGIE'S STORY

Maggie was not a very good housekeeper. Even while the children were still living at home, she had seldom spent much time on her house. Now that the kids were gone and she was occupied by her full-time job, she left most of the work for Mrs. Kennedy, who came in to clean the new condo every Tuesday.

One Saturday morning while her husband, Larry, was out doing some shopping, Maggie decided to tidy up his bed table. She picked up and neatened a pile of books, heaps of old mail, and a stack of old magazines. As she straightened a bunch of car catalogs that Larry had accumulated, one, smaller than the rest, fell out of her hands. Maggie set the now-neat pile down and bent over to pick up the fallen booklet.

As she glanced at the cover, she expected to see a photograph of the latest in Detroit's arsenal. Instead, she gazed at a picture of a woman's voluptuous body, dressed in a revealing red teddy with long red stockings connected to lacy red garters. Maggie stared for a moment at the sensual expression on the woman's face, then she noticed a man's hands, just visible around the woman's waist.

She turned the catalog over and saw that it was addressed to the previous occupants of their condo. Even after six months, the post office was not totally clear on who lived where. Although the number was dwindling, a few pieces of mail, this among them, were still being misdelivered.

Maggie sat down on the edge of the king-sized bed and opened the well-thumbed catalog. She turned page after page of erotic photos of women in expensive, revealing underwear, bodysuits, lounge- and nightwear. In many of the pictures, handsome half-dressed men could be seen taking obvious pleasure in gazing at their ladies.

After looking through the brochure twice, Maggie carefully returned it to the middle of the stack.

Over the next few days, Maggie's mind often strayed to the pictures in the catalog. She could still see the looks on the faces of the men as they gazed at the scantily clad women.

Maggie and Larry had been married for twenty-three years and, until now, she had given little thought to how Larry saw her. She knew that she was not a beautiful woman. She had always wanted to lose twenty pounds but never had. Her face was plain and she had a considerable amount of gray in her hair. But if Larry enjoyed looking at pictures like those in that magazine, maybe he would enjoy looking at her dressed in something sexy. If she could get him to look at her the way those men looked at those models . . .

For weeks, she fought the temptation to buy something from the catalog. That was just what the company wanted women to think, she said to herself. They are in the business of selling lingerie. Of course they posed the pictures that way. They want silly women like me to believe that clothes can make a woman sexy. She thought about her forty-seven-year-old body and shook her head. No way would this unsexy woman look sensual in skimpy underwear. Rather, I would look like an overaged hooker in any of that stuff.

But still, Larry had saved the catalog, and the catalog's position in the stack changed frequently. He obviously looked at it often.

Larry and Maggie's sex life was pleasing to them both, but the teenage passion that they had felt when they first married had cooled over the years. They made love once or twice a week and both seemed satisfied with the arrangement. Larry made an effort to see that Maggie was satisfied, and Maggie did the same. The pressure of their hectic jobs and Larry's ailing parents had taken a toll over the years, however.

Early one afternoon, on an unexpected day off, Maggie withdrew the catalog from the stack and carefully studied it. She selected a particularly revealing black teddy with long black garters and a pair of black stockings with flowers woven into the design.

Maggie realized that if Larry saw the package, the return address would be a dead giveaway. Then she wouldn't be able to change her mind and return the stuff. So she called her sister and asked whether she could have a package delivered to her house. "A surprise for Larry," she told her sister, not elaborating. When they had agreed, Maggie dialed the toll-free number listed in the catalog and ordered the items.

A few weeks later, she picked up the package from her sister's house without satisfying her sister's curiosity about the contents. She'll think I'm some kind of old fool going through menopausal craziness.

That evening, Maggie and Larry were lying in bed, watching a rerun of "T. J. Hooker." Actually, Larry was watching while Maggie agonized about how she was going to arrange the rest of the evening. When she had arrived home, she had been too nervous to open the package. Instead, she had hidden the still-unopened box in the bathroom along with a pair of shoes, just in case. She knew that she'd better either wear the items tonight or send them back. By tomorrow, her courage would be gone.

"I'll just be a minute," she said to Larry, who barely noticed her get up and go into the bathroom. With trembling hands, Maggie unwrapped the box. There they were, the teddy and the stockings. Can I do it? she wondered. Is it worth the risk that he may laugh? Yes! she resolved. It is. And it's now or never.

She pulled off her jeans, shirt, and underwear and put them in the bathroom closet. She slipped the teddy on and almost hoped it wouldn't fit. Then she could send everything back and forget the whole thing. But the teddy closed up the front with long red satin laces and fit just fine.

She deliberately kept her back to the bathroom mirror while she finished dressing. She knew that if she looked at herself, she'd lose her nerve. She slipped on the pair of black high-heeled shoes that she had hidden there earlier. She used only a small hand mirror when she touched up her makeup. Then she quickly sprayed on a bit of cologne and opened the bathroom door. When she emerged, Larry was facing the TV, his back to her.

"Larry," she said softly. "I bought something that I'd like your opinion on."

"Sure, honey," Larry said without looking up from his program.

"You have to look," she said, her heart pounding. If he laughs . . .

Larry turned, and the expression on his face made all of Maggie's nervousness worthwhile. He just stared, his eyes wandering over her body. His mouth moved as if to say something, but no words came out.

Maggie placed her hands on her hips and said softly, "Do you like the outfit?"

Larry continued to stare.

"I guess that means you like it," she said.

"It looks w-w-wonderful," Larry said, his eyes never leaving her body. "Whatever possessed you?"

Maggie ignored his question. "Would you like to

touch?" she asked. She had no idea what had come over her. She felt like a temptress.

Her eyes never left Larry's face as she walked slowly over to the bed. As her husband reached up to touch the black satiny fabric, Maggie leaned over and pressed the Off button on the TV's remote control. As she leaned, she brushed the tips of her lace-covered breasts across Larry's chest. She sat down on the edge of the bed as Larry ran trembling fingers over the sides of the teddy.

"Feel the stockings," Maggie suggested. "They are so silky."

Larry grazed his fingertips over the nylon and felt the heat from her legs underneath. Maggie took his hands and ran them up and down the garters, then lifted them to the lace over the breasts.

I've never seen him look at me like this, she thought. As she held his hand, she realized that his palm was damp and his breathing was uneven.

She held Larry's hand and brushed his palm over her breasts. Her nipples swelled as he stroked the lace. She dropped her hands as Larry continued to caress her body beneath the teddy.

Without a word, Larry pulled Maggie down next to him and aggressively pressed his mouth against hers. His tongue tore her mouth open and plundered, reaching and touching everywhere inside. His kiss made her breathless.

He pulled the teddy's straps off her shoulders and pushed the fabric down to expose her breasts. He took one of her breasts in each hand and squeezed. He pressed his mouth first to one, then the other, alternately kissing and sucking each nipple. He was crazy for her. Maggie now understood the meaning of the word *lust,* and Larry's lust was directed at her. She let her body go with the new sensations.

Larry reached for the soaked crotch of the teddy and pulled the snaps open. His fingers drove inside her wet cunt, plunging and withdrawing until her hips joined his rhythm.

With one hand, he unzipped his pants and pulled his huge erection free. Still almost fully dressed, he rolled on top of Maggie and drove his cock hard into her wetness. It was only a moment until, with a shout, he came.

He surfaced and realized that she was not yet satisfied. He fondled her clitoris the way he knew she liked, gradually increasing the speed of his stroking.

"Oh God," she said, "don't stop! Please don't stop!"

"Don't worry," he whispered. "I have no intention of stopping." He found her rhythm and felt her swell even more under his hand.

It was only moments until she climaxed, waves of pleasure engulfing her.

Later he said, "I'm sorry it was so fast. That outfit made me crazy." Then he asked, "How did you know?"

She slipped her hand into the stack of magazines and withdrew the catalog.

Larry looked embarrassed. "I never imagined it

would excite me so much to see you wear that outfit. God, you're beautiful."

Maggie knew she was not beautiful, but it didn't matter. "I'm only sorry I didn't buy an outfit like this sooner." She held the catalog up and opened to the first page. "Would you help me pick out another one?"

Within a month, Maggie had a large wardrobe of sensual underthings that she wore frequently. Larry sometimes secretly bought special items, wrapped them, and presented them to his wife with great ceremony. Their lovemaking took on a whole new aspect.

They had a particularly enjoyable evening one Saturday. As they were dressing to go to dinner with friends, Maggie allowed Larry to touch her white lace half bra and matching tiny panties. Then she pushed him away and quickly pulled on her slacks and sweater. Larry could barely wait to get her home.

For Larry's birthday, Maggie picked out a specially outrageous one-piece see-through jumpsuit. The night of his birthday, she put the jumpsuit on and tied a wide red ribbon around her waist. As he untied the ribbon, she said, "Since I am giving myself to you, let's just call this outfit Gift Wrap."

I learned early in my sexual life how difficult it was to discuss what I liked or what I wanted my partner to do. During sex, it was almost impossible for me to say something as simple as "Could you do that again?" much less "Could you do that differently?" I think back now and lament. My sex life as a young-married could have been so much richer and more rewarding for both myself and my husband had either of us been able to talk before, during, or after sex. In the later years of my marriage, I thought about trying to discuss how to attempt the kind of sex I read about in books, but old habits die hard.

Throughout my relationships, I have used body language to suggest different positions or activities and so has my partner. The suggestions that I have made this way have been properly interpreted about half the time and I'm sure that I've interpreted my partner's actions with about the same success. You probably know the signals, subtle though they may be, that your partner sends during lovemaking when she wants a certain type of touching or a particular position.

When it comes to new adventures, physical reactions can be very instructive if you are tuned in. Dave discovered his wife Judy's favorite sexual fantasy during an ordinary outing to a local movie. Fortunately for both of them, Dave was tuned in to Judy's nonverbal clues and he was willing to take a big risk and try something creative.

DAVE AND JUDY'S STORY

Dave and Judy sat midway back in the darkened theater. After about an hour, Dave started to shift restlessly in his seat.

Why did I let Judy talk me into seeing this turkey? he wondered. She knows that I don't like war movies.

The film was a recent remake of a 1942 World War II movie, updated with R-rated scenes filled with blood and sex. The plot was predictable. The beautiful Nazi spy, played by a voluptuous brunette, had been trying to get some top-secret plans from the hero. Now she had fallen in love with the handsome flier and was being taken to task by her superiors.

"We are holding your sister," the actor said in a poor imitation of a German accent. The Nazi officer led the heroine down a set of old stone stairs to the basement of the château.

The picture changed to a shot of a small dungeon-type room, where the heroine was looking through a small barred window. Her sister was standing half-clothed on the far side of the room, with her back against the stones and her wrists spread over her head, tied to rings in the wall. A

Nazi lieutenant with tall, shiny boots marched back and forth in front of her and taunted her with lewd accounts of what he would do with her if her sister, the spy, didn't cooperate.

Suddenly, Dave realized that Judy's grip on his hand had tightened. Her hand shook and her palm was sweaty. He turned and looked at his wife. Although Judy's face was illuminated only by the light from the movie screen, Dave could see that it was flushed and her lips were slightly parted. She stared at the girl who was tied to the wall and being teased by the lieutenant with the shiny boots.

Dave had never seen his wife like this, except when she was very excited in bed. He leaned over and whispered into her ear.

"Do you like what you see?" he asked.

Dave's only indication that she might have heard him was an increase in Judy's breathing rate.

She didn't answer because she was lost somewhere between the theater and a cell in Germany, but she didn't have to answer aloud. Her face and body language told it all.

Dave and Judy had always been adventurous in bed, but nothing like what he was watching had ever occurred to him. He had read stories and letters in magazines about women who like to be sexually dominated, and the idea interested and aroused him, but it had never occurred to him that Judy might enjoy it. Even in play, is sex about domination? He didn't want to use force to insist, just to enhance.

Dave wanted to be sure there was no mistake. He leaned over and placed his mouth close to Judy's ear. "The guard is going to punish his prisoner," he murmured, "and there's nothing she can do about it. She's helpless." Judy trembled and her breathing was ragged.

As he watched her face, Dave realized that he was as excited as she was by the scene that played out on the screen. He glanced back and forth from the screen to his wife's face. Yes, he admitted to himself, he wanted to see his wife tied up, at his mercy, and it was reasonably clear that she wanted it, too.

Dave vowed to make it happen, somehow. He knew that it was a risk, but he was sure that he'd know if he was wrong. He could read his wife very well. If anything went too far, he would know it or Judy would tell him, somehow.

It was almost a week before Dave got the opportunity to act out what he and Judy had seen in the movie.

It was a cold Sunday in January. Their ten-year-old twins were out for the entire afternoon. Dave and Judy often took advantage of a time like this and spent it in bed. Dave suggested that they go upstairs and lock the door, and Judy agreed immediately.

In the bedroom, Judy sat down on the bed and Dave lit a fire in the small freestanding fireplace he had installed a year earlier. Then he sat down next to Judy.

As they lay back on the bed, Dave began to

stroke Judy's face the way he knew she enjoyed. He stroked her hair as she rested her head on his chest. He felt her whole body relax.

He kissed her softly and felt her mouth open under his. The tip of his tongue explored her lips, delaying his penetration of her open mouth. Then, gradually, he slid his tongue between her teeth and stroked the roof of her mouth. He felt her tongue play with his, swirling and sliding over it.

He twisted her long dark hair around one hand and pulled gently. He held her head back, with her neck arched. He felt her reaction immediately. Her body started to move under his and her arms wrapped tightly around his shoulders. He was right. Why had he never noticed this reaction before?

He reached down and slowly pulled up Judy's sweater while he stroked her ribs. Her eyes were closed and her lips were parted. Her breathing was quick and uneven.

He had planned the afternoon carefully and the knowledge of what was to come was making him incredibly hungry. Dave used both hands and, with one movement, he pulled the sweater up over Judy's head and threw it across the room. Then he reached behind her, unhooked her bra, pulled it off, and hurled it after her sweater.

He loved her breasts. They were small, with very little flesh. As he ran his hands over her chest, he could almost feel her ribs through the flesh, except for where her large nipples and aureoles colored and softened her body. He started to flick his tongue over her skin. He planted butterfly kisses on her sides and along her ribs. He ran his tongue down to her navel, which just showed over the waist of her jeans.

He pushed her back until she lay full length on the bed. Without any thought, she stretched her arms above her head and crossed her wrists. He had seen her this way many times, but he had never made the connection before. There was no doubt in his mind now. She wanted to be helpless as much as he wanted it.

Her nipples stood out from her chest and he knew that she was very excited. It was time for him to act. Earlier in the day, he had tied silk scarves to the four corners of the bed frame. Now he used one hand to pull one out and, with his free hand, he grabbed one of Judy's wrists and held it tightly.

As he wrapped the scarf around her wrist, Judy's eyes flew open. She held her breath and trembled.

"Don't argue," Dave said. "We're going to do this my way."

A tiny smile played around Judy's mouth. "I have no intention of arguing," she said huskily.

Dave quickly tied the scarf to her wrist. He slowly got up off the bed, walked around, and pulled out the scarf on the other side. Judy hadn't moved and didn't resist as he quickly tied her other wrist.

He looked at her, briefly serious. "You can always holler uncle if you want." "Holler uncle" had always been their code word for "I really want to stop." Judy nodded.

"Don't hurt me," Judy said with a tiny whimper.

Dave smiled. She was clearly getting into the spirit of what was going on.

"I won't hurt you, my dear," he said, "as long as you cooperate." He almost used a German accent, but he didn't think he could without laughing.

Dave reached down and pulled off Judy's shoes and socks. Then he unbuttoned her jeans and pulled them, together with her underpants, over her hips and down off of her ankles.

"Yes," he said. "Very lovely." She had never looked more beautiful or more erotic. He quickly tied her ankles to the two lower corners of the bed with slipknots. He wanted to be able to free her quickly later, if he wanted to.

She was his now and there was nothing she could do about it. Judy closed her eyes, eager to experience what was coming next.

Dave walked to the side of the bed and sat down. He leaned over and, without warning, bit her nipple gently. Judy jumped and tried to pull away, but she could do nothing. Her bonds were secure. Dave held her nipple between his teeth and pulled and sucked.

Judy's hips moved restlessly, searching for something that she couldn't reach. She stayed in character. "Please don't," she begged. "I'm a good girl, a nice girl."

Finally, Dave sat up and ran his finger through the curls between her legs. "I don't think you're a nice girl at all." He stroked her again. "Nice girls don't get so wet."

Slowly, he stood up and, with great deliberation,

he removed his shirt. Judy watched him, her eyes blazing with desire. He stripped very slowly, enjoying the way his wife's eyes followed his fingers as he undid his buttons and unzipped his fly.

As his erection sprang from his shorts, Judy unconsciously opened her mouth. She had always been willing to use her mouth on him, but it was always because she knew he liked it. Now she could think of nothing but how much she wanted his huge cock to fill her mouth. The roles they were playing didn't permit her to say so, but she could ask in another way.

"You wouldn't make me suck that thing," she said, and stared at his penis.

Dave smiled. He bent over and stroked her face with his hand. He ran the tip of his thumb across her lips, then gently forced her mouth open and inserted his index finger. She sucked on it as though it were his penis. He pulled his finger out and pushed it in several times, imitating the thrusting of his cock.

When he could wait no longer, he wound his hand in her hair and twisted her face toward his belly. He pressed the tip of his cock against her mouth and pushed it in. She sucked him like a wild animal, swirling her tongue around and around. She drew him to the back of her throat, then pulled her head back so he slipped almost all the way out. The torture of her sucking was too much for Larry. He tangled his fingers in the back of Judy's hair and rammed his cock deep into her sucking mouth over and over.

It was incredibly exciting for both of them. Dave quickly realized that if he didn't stop, he was going to come in her mouth, and that wasn't what he had in mind at all.

He yanked her hair and pulled her mouth away. "Enough," he said roughly.

Judy smiled briefly before slipping back into her role. "I'm a good girl," she whined. "Don't make me do these terrible things."

"You don't have any choice, do you?" Dave pulled at the scarf that held one wrist.

"No," Judy said simply.

While he calmed down a bit, Dave kissed and teased his helpless wife for many minutes until she was writhing and reaching for him with her body. Her arms and legs strained at the silken restraints.

"Now, my dear," he said, "I'm going to prove that you're not a good girl. I know you want me." He wrapped his hand around his cock and stroked her wet cunt with it.

"You want me, don't you?"

Judy said nothing. The girl she was playing wouldn't have admitted anything.

"Tell me you want me." He continued to rub her cunt with his cock and watch her face. Her body was covered with a thin sheen of perspiration and he could tell from her expression when she was close to coming. He backed off, raising his body on his elbows and knees so none of his skin touched hers.

He watched as she caught her breath. He was in complete control and he wanted Judy to beg to be fucked. The Nazi officer in the film would have made the heroine beg, and now Dave wanted to hear his wife do the same.

When she had quieted, he brushed her hot cunt with his penis. He stroked her slowly, watching her hips move to meet him.

"You have to tell me that you want me." He smiled as she watched. "I have all day and I can keep this up indefinitely. You won't get what you need until you ask for it."

Judy looked at Dave's face and saw that he meant what he said. He would keep teasing her until she said what he wanted. She almost wanted him to keep teasing her, but his stroking was making her crazy with need.

Finally, she whispered, "I want you."

"I can't hear you."

"I want you," she said louder.

"Beg!" he snapped.

Judy was silent. Dave pressed just the tip of his penis into her vagina. He pulled it out and repeated the process. He was fucking her with just the tip of his cock.

"Beg!"

"Please," Judy said.

"Please what?" Dave said, still fucking her with just the tip of his cock.

"Please fuck me," Judy whimpered. "Fuck me good."

With one motion, Dave thrust his huge erection deep between Judy's widespread legs. Again and again, he thrust into her until he felt her climax. As she came, so did he.

Without withdrawing, Dave reached around and pulled open the slipknot that held each of Judy's legs. Immediately, she wrapped her legs around his waist and held him tight inside of her.

Sweat cooled on their bodies, and, as their breathing slowed, Dave reached up and untied Judy's wrists. Then he pulled the quilt over them and they stayed together.

When the children got home, Dave called, "Get your own dinner. Your mother and I may not come out 'til morning."

Judy giggled and snuggled closer.

Then there was Tracy, who correctly interpreted her husband Paul's unspoken request.

TRACY AND PAUL'S STORY

Tracy was an average-looking twenty-six-year-old woman who did her best to look anything but average. She had curly black hair that she wore short so that it formed a small cloud around her head. She frequently wore huge earrings that hung down to her shoulders. Her makeup highlighted her large brown eyes and smooth skin and she wore clothes that accentuated her figure, but she never really felt good about the way she looked.

Tracy's banker husband, Paul, was twenty-seven and attractive enough that Tracy occasionally became jealous at parties when some woman paid too much attention to him. He was six feet tall and worked out at least twice a week to keep his almost two-hundred-pound body firm.

Tracy and Paul had been married for five years. Before they were married, their sex life had been great, but after the ceremony, Paul's lovemaking became routine. A year earlier, Tracy had been tempted to have a brief affair with a handsome man she met at work, but, in the age of AIDS, she was afraid to indulge her desires. More recently, Paul had spent a weekend at a convention and, after a long evening of partying, had ended up in bed with a sexy conventioneer from another state. Other than those brief encounters, Paul and Tracy had been monogamous.

One afternoon, Tracy and Paul and another couple, Sarah and Gil, went to the beach. They walked down to an area where there were only a few other people, spread their blanket, and dropped their belongings. Tracy pulled off her T-shirt and shorts and sat down next to her husband.

As she sat, she became aware that Paul's eyes were riveted on Sarah, who was slowly unbuttoning her blouse. As Gil egged her on, she did a slow striptease, taking almost five minutes to reveal her skimpy bikini. As Tracy looked down at the bulge in the front of Paul's trunks, she couldn't misread his reaction.

As they lay in bed that evening, Tracy hesitantly said, "I was watching you as Sarah slowly took off her clothes today. Did it excite you as much as I think it did?"

Paul was a bit embarrassed by the question, but he answered truthfully, "Yeah, I guess it did."

"Did you ever go to a strip show?" Tracy asked.

Paul sighed and gazed at the ceiling. "Once, some years ago, some of us went to a topless bar after work. The stripping was real ritualized. You know, three girls each took off their clothes at the same time. Each of them looked bored. One actually looked annoyed at the customers for being there and making her bother with it all." His eyes closed as he momentarily lost himself in the memory.

Tracy waited silently and hoped he would continue.

After a few moments, he opened his eyes and looked at his wife. "I guess I have to admit that it was very exciting in spite of everything," he said. "Today, at the beach, just watching a woman slowly exposing herself . . ."

Tracy leaned over and kissed him.

They made love again in the morning. It seemed to Tracy that just talking about that scene improved their sex life.

The more Tracy thought about Paul's reaction, the more she became intrigued by the idea of helping him act out this bit of fantasy. She wasn't sure that when the time came she would be able to carry it off, but, judging from Paul's ardor, it would be worth the effort.

About a week later, she was ready to try. She arranged for each of the children to be away overnight. She cooked a special dinner and served a bottle of white wine. She wasn't sure whether the wine was to improve Paul's mood or to give her courage, but it did both.

While Paul went into the living room and settled in front of the television, Tracy went into the bedroom and changed into the outfit she had planned over the past week. It had been exciting just buying the different pieces, each in a different store. She had hunted for the shoes for three days.

She finished her makeup and checked her image in the full-length mirror on the back of the bathroom door. It was the first time she had seen the entire outfit and she was startled at the different woman who looked back at her. Could she be that person? What the hell, she said to herself. Nothing ventured, nothing gained. And she did have quite a bit to gain. She took a deep breath, went back into the living room, and sat in a chair across from Paul. She demurely crossed her legs.

"You changed your clothes," Paul said as he glanced up from the TV. Tracy was now wearing a tight black skirt with a long slit up one side. She had on a white blouse that closed up the front with fifteen buttons, only ten of which were buttoned, black stockings, and black shoes with five-inch spike heels.

"And you look . . . different." Paul's eyes wandered over her body.

She had put her makeup on differently, with more drama around the eyes. Her lipstick was a deep shade of red, which matched the shade she had used on her nails. "Do you like the look?" she asked seductively.

"Yeah, I do. You look great. Are you going to come over and sit next to me while we watch the movie?" Paul patted the cushion next to him as he began hesitantly to describe the movie he had intended to watch. His eyes never left Tracy's body.

While he talked, Tracy began to run her finger up and down her neck as she played with her large golden hoop earrings. As her fingers moved idly, they strayed to her chest and one finger slid into the valley between her breasts. Gradually she became aware that Paul had stopped talking and was just watching her finger stroke up and down the center of her chest. She loved the feeling of his eyes on her, of having his undivided attention.

She reached over and picked up her wineglass and sipped a bit. She swallowed and then ran her tongue around her lips, very slowly.

She uncrossed and recrossed her legs, allowing the slit to fall open. Tracy had always been proud of her long, shapely legs, which were shown off to their best advantage in her black stockings.

As she watched Paul's eyes, darkened with lust,

caress her legs, she was suddenly very turned on. It felt like a stranger was watching her do something very bad.

She reached up and unbuttoned three more buttons. She had bought a lacy white bra that hooked in the front. She had deliberately bought it one cup size too small so that it pushed her breasts up and deepened her cleavage.

"I've never seen you like this, Tracy," Paul said as he licked his lips.

At that moment, Tracy was afraid that he would add something that would break the spell and she would lose her nerve, but all he said was, "I like what I see."

Tracy could feel her nipples harden under Paul's scrutiny and they pressed against the cups of her bra. She continued to unbutton her blouse until it fell open. Paul was staring at her breasts, which spilled out of the tight lace.

Tracy sat up and leaned forward to give Paul a better view while she removed the blouse. Then she dropped it on the floor. She sipped her wine as Paul's eyes looked her over from head to foot.

On a whim, she took the chilled glass and ran it over her upper chest and across her upper abdomen. The cold was very erotic and the moisture from the outside of the glass made her skin shine. She put the glass down and used her fingertips to spread the film of moisture around her abdomen and ribs.

Paul reached for his glass and took a long drink,

but his eyes never left Tracy's fingers as they wandered over her skin.

She recrossed her legs and her skirt rode still higher. A thin line of pink flesh was now exposed above the tops of her stockings.

"You never wore stockings like that before," Paul said hoarsely.

"I never did a lot of things before," Tracy said. The line sounded corny, but Paul didn't seem to mind. He just continued to stare.

After a moment, Tracy reached down and unhooked the bra. She let it fall open, but her breasts remained in the cups. She watched Paul's hands as he idly ran his fingers over the rough fabric on the sofa. It was as though his fingers craved sensation, any sensation.

Slowly, Tracy's fingers danced up and down between her breasts until finally her thumb and index finger grasped one cup of her bra. She saw that Paul was holding his breath. She took a long time to pull the cup to the side and expose her breast.

Her nipples were hard and swollen. She fondled her breast and gently pinched and pulled at the nipple. Paul's eyes never left her fingers. It was as if he had never seen her before.

Tracy rested her head against the back of the chair as she duplicated her motions with her other hand on her other breast.

She leaned forward and pulled the bra off. Paul shifted his position and Tracy watched the small movement as he adjusted his slacks to a more comfortable position.

With one hand, she continued to stroke her breast while she rested the other on her knee. She slowed the motion on her breast and ran her fingers up the inside of her thigh, just to the top of her stocking. Then she stroked back down to her knee again.

Paul's eyes flicked back and forth from the hand on her thigh to the one on her breast.

"More?" Tracy asked softly. She knew the answer but wanted affirmation from Paul.

He could only nod.

Tracy stood up. After two pregnancies, she had lost pride in her breasts. They sagged more than she wished, but now, watching Paul's face, she raised her elbows and looked down. She could see her large nipples, dark brown and more swollen than she could ever remember.

She looked back at Paul. Whatever complaint she had with her reflection in her mirror, she had no complaint with her reflection in her husband's eyes.

Her skirt had buttons from the top of the slit to the waist. One by one, she opened the buttons until only her hands kept the skirt wrapped around her waist.

"Yes?" she asked.

"Please," Paul said.

She gently let the skirt fall to the floor. She had bought a pair of black lace panties, which covered the black garter belt that held up her stockings.

Tracy could see the big bulge in the front of Paul's slacks. She loved the idea that she had caused it without ever touching him.

She inserted her thumbs under the waistband of her panties, but Paul said breathlessly, "Not yet."

He stood up and took out his wallet. He pulled out a ten-dollar bill and sat back down. He reached out and rubbed the bill up the inside of Tracy's thigh. Then he tucked it into the top of one stocking.

She was now a paid stripper, a pro. The thought made her even wetter, hungrier for Paul. But a stripper should give a complete show. Agonizingly slowly, she again hooked her thumbs inside the waistband of her panties and pulled them down an inch at a time.

It took several long minutes for her pants to join her blouse, skirt, and bra on the floor at her feet.

When she started to unhook the garters from the stockings, Paul whispered, "Leave them on. I want to make love to you that way."

Paul stood up and put one arm around Tracy's shoulders. His other hand was on her breast, squeezing her nipple. "Come upstairs," he said, his voice barely audible.

They walked up to the bedroom and Tracy sat on the edge of the bed. Dressed only in the garter belt, stockings, and shoes, she leaned back on her elbows while Paul undressed. Her curly dark pubic hair showed clearly below the garter belt.

As Paul pulled down his slacks and underpants, Tracy saw that his cock was enormous.

Paul stood in front of her, naked. He reached down and grasped his penis. "See what you did?" he said hoarsely. "You made me want you."

"And I want *you*," Tracy said, spreading her thighs.

Paul sat down on the bed next to her as she lay back. He leaned down and put his mouth around her nipple as he slid his hand between her legs.

Tracy closed her eyes. Somehow, it feels like I'm making love to a stranger, someone who paid me to strip and has now bought me for the evening. The feeling of this stranger's fingers stroking the wet flesh between her legs made her so hot.

Tracy grasped her husband's throbbing penis. She put the tip against her wet vagina and pressed upward with her hips. Without any hesitation, he quickly rolled her over on top of him and pressed her into a sitting position. With one motion, he lifted her and set her down on his immense penis.

She kicked off her shoes and pressed her stockinged legs against his sides. She used Paul's flanks to stroke the insides of her thighs through the silky nylon.

She alternately lifted her hips and then ground them against Paul as he thrust upward into her over and over. His fingers dug into the flesh at her waist and he pressed her more tightly onto his cock.

"It's so good," she cried. "You feel so good inside of me."

He could feel her lacy garter belt under his fingers. "God, I'm going to come deep inside of you," he screamed, and he poured his semen inside of her.

With a sigh, she collapsed on top of him and wrapped her arms around his heaving chest. She placed her cheek against his nipples and listened as his heart pounded.

They slept pressed tightly together. When they woke the next morning, Tracy remembered that she still had her stockings and garter belt on. As she started to get up to remove them, Paul said simply, "Not yet, my little stripper."

They didn't get up for another hour.

4

FIRST TIMES

I've discussed some ways to introduce new sexual activities. Now the question becomes "Like what?" I've already mentioned a few. Maggie discovered the power of lingerie and Dave and Judy found that control was a key to their excitement. Are there things for everyone? I think so.

Until recently, it was believed that men and women had different and frequently incompatible sexual needs. Mother told daughter and the media reinforced the myth. As a child, I was told that men have a physical drive that makes them want, indeed need, sex more often than women. A woman must never deny her husband his "marital rights." If you're not in the mood, oh well. Make the best of it and pretend to enjoy yourself so you won't wound his delicate male ego. It may not have ever been spelled out in exactly those words, but the message was clear nonetheless.

The message in the fifties, when I was a teen-

59

ager, was that while men do need variation in their sexual encounters, that's what prostitutes and "other women" are for. Foreplay was not enjoyable in and of itself. It was a means to an end, a way to excite one or both partners so intercourse would not be too odious. Wives were supposed to be vessels, repositories for the seed of their husbands, and content with the missionary position. Many men never saw their wives naked. Lovemaking took place with all the lights off and with the wife's nightclothes still on. Then the men went out and had fun elsewhere.

At least men were taught that sex was fun!

Now, fortunately, it is more commonly understood that women have sexual needs and desires, too. They have erotic fantasies and their own type of wet dreams. They masturbate and have enjoyable orgasms. Women can and should enjoy sex, too, in all its infinite varieties. Sex is to be shared, enjoyed mutually by both partners. Sex is fun for both participants. Hooray for enlightenment!

It's all right to want whatever you want and that includes games that are out of the sexual mainstream. Once you accept that what you want is all right, you have to communicate these new ideas with your partner.

Sexual creativity is a most important ingredient in a long-term, full-time relationship. I used to think that the perfect sexual partner was someone with infinite creativity. I hoped that there was someone out there who could enjoy the same pleasures that I enjoy. I also foolishly thought that he would be able to divine what I wished and do it just right. I never considered how he would know all this; I just knew that, when I found him, he would.

I was wrong. The perfect partner is one with whom you can communicate. One to whom you can suggest activities that you might like to try. One who can say, "That sounds interesting," or "I don't think I'd enjoy that," with equal equanimity. One who can suggest things to you and will accept your response, whatever it may be.

A perfect new sexual experience, the first time with someone who really turns you on, is the basis of many sexual fantasies. In the next two stories, you'll see how two quite different couples reacted to that initial delicious awkwardness. Maybe you'd enjoy marking one of these.

PEGGY AND GARY'S STORY

Gary lay stretched out on the bed, a copy of the newspaper propped on his heavy thighs. Contentedly, he turned to the last page and spent several leisurely minutes reading about his high school lacrosse team's latest victory. Nostalgically, he thought about the days before his waistline thickened and his hair thinned. He remembered the "big game," in which he had actually played only two minutes but which, over the years, had become his greatest triumph.

With a dreamy look on his face, he put his newspaper aside and glanced at Peggy, his wife of almost twenty years, as she lay beside him. He smiled at the way she lay, almost prone, with her head on her scrunched pillow. Every few moments, she absently pushed her glasses back up to the bridge of her nose. He looked at the cover of the paperback novel she was reading.

"Why do the covers of all the books you read look the same?"

Absently, Peggy looked up. "Were you talking to me?" she asked.

"I was just wondering about the covers on those novels you read. They all look alike."

Peggy looked at the cover of her book. It showed the handsome, virile hero bent over the lush body of the heroine. He was shirtless, showing off his rippling chest and shoulder muscles. She wore a gown, cut low enough to leave little of her full breasts to the imagination. Her red hair was spread over her shoulders in deep, thick waves. The lovers gazed into each other's eyes, oblivious to the rest of the world.

Peggy looked at the cover illustration and giggled. "I guess they all do look alike."

"Why?" When Peggy looked puzzled, Gary continued. "Why do you read the same book over and over? Granted, the characters have different names and the setting is different, but the story is always the same. I've always wondered. What's the real appeal?"

"Romance, I guess," Peggy answered after a bit of thought. "I suppose I read them because there's always romance. My favorite part is when the hero finally makes love to the heroine for the first time. He holds her and kisses her and drives her wild with passion. She usually wants to resist him for some reason, but she finds herself unable to. His expert lovemaking ultimately wins her over."

She rolled partway over and propped herself on one elbow. "Like the scene I just read." She turned back a few pages and handed the book to Gary. "Read from here," she said, and pointed to a paragraph.

Five minutes later, Gary handed the book back. Reading that scene had turned him on more than he would have imagined. "I see what you mean. It's very erotic, like an orgasm in print."

He wanted to be the man in the story. He wanted to be able to reduce a woman to a quivering mass of desire. He wondered whether he could do that to Peggy or whether he even dared to try. The idea was too tempting to ignore.

"We could make love like that," he said softly.

Peggy thought about her recent lovemaking with Gary. It was comfortable, but predictable. She would love it if he could behave like one of the heroes of the novels she loved so much. But the whole idea was ridiculous.

"Real people don't make love like that," she said.

Gary reached over and took the book from

Peggy's hand. Without a word, he put it on his bed table. He turned back to Peggy and ran his fingers over her forehead, then took off her glasses, folded them, and placed them on her bedstand.

In the story, the hero and the heroine had just married, over the heroine's objections. "I'm going to make love to you, since this is our wedding night." That was the first line in the scene and Gary tried to say it as the hero would have.

He swallowed hard and held his breath. What would Peggy do? After a moment's hesitation, Peggy pulled her knees up slightly and backed away toward her side of the bed. "But it's early yet. Maybe you'd prefer a glass of wine. I could get one for you." Gary's heart pounded. Peggy had just repeated the heroine's line.

"I promise I won't hurt you," Gary continued. He slid out of his side of the bed and took off the top of his pajamas. He stood for a moment, wearing only the pajama pants.

As Peggy looked at him, she saw the same nice guy she had been sleeping next to for twenty years. He was a bit paunchy and his hairline had receded so far that he was soon going to have to admit that he was bald. She noticed also that he had broad shoulders, long arms, and beautiful hands.

In another part of her mind, however, he was Bret, the hero of the novel. He was about to ravish the teenage girl he had just forced to marry him. Peggy worried that, as much as she wanted to become Leona, the heroine, she couldn't become a sweet, beautiful, sexually ignorant girl. Gary would laugh.

As she looked at his face, though, she saw the languid look that she had always read about, the look that made his eyes say, I want to seduce you.

"I'm afraid," she said, as she thought Leona would have.

Gary climbed back onto the bed. "Don't be afraid," he said. "You will want it as much as I do. Just relax and let me love you."

Gary touched Peggy's face with the tips of his fingers. As his wife gazed at him, he stroked her chin and cheeks. He softly touched her eyelids and she closed her eyes.

"You really are beautiful," he said. There was such sincerity in his voice that Peggy didn't know whether it was Bret talking to Leona or Gary talking to his wife. She didn't want to know. She just wanted to enjoy.

She felt Gary place tiny kisses on her temple and then his lips wandered over her face. The moment was wonderful, but Peggy felt a hunger to have Gary's lips on her mouth. She reached for the back of his head to press his mouth against hers.

"Leona," he said, "you're very forward." He was gently reminding her that, in the scene, Leona had been totally passive, frightened of lovemaking until Bret was actually inside of her. Peggy dropped her hand.

Gary continued to kiss her face. He enjoyed denying her the kiss she obviously wanted. He kissed her ear and ran the tip of his tongue around the outside. As he heard Peggy purr, he moved to her neck. He placed a line of light kisses down the side of her neck to where her neck met her shoulder. As he nibbled at that tender spot, he felt her reach her body toward him.

Gently, he reached for the back of her hair and pulled her away. He saw the pleasure on her face as he bent to touch his lips to hers. To his delight, she didn't open her mouth immediately but kept her lips together as the girl in the story had. He kissed her closed mouth and then ran the tip of his tongue over her lips. Gradually, her lips parted just enough for him to slip his tongue inside.

It was heavenly. Somehow it was like Bret kissing Leona. Gary enjoyed Peggy's kiss as he hadn't in many years. They kissed for a long time, exploring each other's mouths for the "first time."

Gary's hands kneaded Peggy's lower back. He cupped her buttocks and pressed her belly against his erection so she could feel the heat of his excitement.

They separated just enough for him to slide his hand onto her breasts. She stiffened as Leona would have, but he said, "It's all right, darling, just relax." Through her nightgown, he kneaded her flesh and rubbed his palm across her swollen nipple. She was trying to react like an innocent, but her body responded like a woman.

After minutes of just playing with her breast, he said, "Doesn't that feel good?"

"Oh, yes," she said hesitantly, "it feels wonderful."

"There are more pleasures," he said as he continued to play out the scene.

Peggy opened her eyes and looked at him. She used body language to convey the fright that Leona would have felt in bed with her handsome new husband. She shuddered, then said, "I'm still frightened."

"Trust me."

Her lips curved in a tiny "I'll be brave" smile and she closed her eyes.

Gary pulled his wife's nightgown off over her head and tossed it on the floor. Then he bent over and touched Peggy's nipple with his tongue. He felt her pull back, but one arm held her tightly. His lips encircled her breast's erect peak and he started to suck. When he squeezed her other nipple in a rhythm that matched his sucking, she moaned.

Hesitantly, Peggy reached up and ran the palms of her hands over the backs of Gary's shoulders. She felt the length of his body against her and his sucking made her wet with need, but still she continued to control herself and behave as Leona would have.

Gary stopped squeezing and sucking, slid his hand down her belly, and slipped his fingers between her legs. She couldn't stop her hips from moving or her back from arching as she reached for him. His hard penis against her thigh told her that he was as excited as she was, but they both were still playing out the scene.

He played with the soaked flesh between her legs until neither of them could resist any longer.

He climbed on top and, with one motion, pressed his hard cock inside. He thrust in and out and watched the pleasure on his wife's face. Her eyes were tightly shut and her head thrashed from side to side.

He pounded into her and climaxed with a groan.

They lay together for a long time as their breathing returned to normal.

"You know," Peggy said, her grin lighting her face, "that should have been silly. But it was wonderful. I was Leona and you were Bret. I can't really explain it."

"It was wonderful, wasn't it?" Gary said, feeling a little silly, too.

"It was strange," Peggy continued. "I almost felt the delicious anticipation of a woman's first experience. I guess I was too young and too hungry to enjoy it this way the first time we made love."

"It seems that we can enjoy all kinds of things in ways we never suspected," Gary said. "I have a few ideas of my own."

PHIL'S STORY

It had been a summer that everyone would remember, especially Phil. Most people would remember the relentless heat that turned New York into an oven. There were endless days with temperatures over ninety and sky-high humidity. Late-afternoon thunderstorms provided no relief.

Though it had been twenty years earlier, Phil would remember that summer forever, not for the heat but because of Mrs. Johnstone. Through the ensuing years, whenever the weather turned hot and humid, he would be transported back to the summer when he was twenty and a junior at college, and his cock would harden.

School let out the last week of May that summer and there was little for him to do. He worked three days a week in the stockroom of the local appliance store, moving heavy boxes containing luxurious air conditioners his family couldn't afford. Once or twice a week, he went to the local movie or borrowed a friend's car and took a girl for a drive away from the heat of the city. In the cool of the suburbs, they would sit in the car and make out. Sometimes he would "hit a home run" and get to put his excited cock inside of the girl, but, most often, he would end the evening frustrated. The rest of the days he hung out on the stoop with his friends. They drank cold beer and prayed for an end to the stifling temperatures.

Late one afternoon in mid-July, Mrs. Johnstone, Phil's upstairs neighbor, staggered home carrying three heavy bundles from the local grocery store and two cans of paint.

Mrs. Johnstone was a nice lady whom everyone in the neighborhood liked. She was forty-five, with a few gray streaks already in her hair and deep smile lines around her mouth. She had lived alone in her third-floor apartment since her husband died.

Phil watched her put her packages down and fumble in her pocketbook for her key, so Phil offered to help with the packages.

"Thank you so much, Phil," Mrs. Johnstone said. "You're such a nice, polite young man."

When they got to her door, Mrs. Johnstone invited Phil in for some cold milk and a slice of freshly baked chocolate cake.

"You know, Phil," Mrs. Johnstone said as they ate, "I'm planning to paint the apartment next week. I wonder whether you'd be interested in helping me. You could move furniture, paint, and help me clean up. I'd pay you, of course."

"It'd be okay, I guess. What would I do?" He didn't have to be at work any day the following week and the extra money would be great.

"I know you work at the appliance store and you must be used to doing all that lifting. You would be a lot of help moving furniture and painting. I couldn't pay you very much. Maybe twenty-five dollars for the three days."

Phil thought about the car he could borrow and the girls he could entertain with the money. "Sure, Mrs. Johnstone, that'd be great."

"It's a deal then. We'll start on Monday. But you have to start calling me Angie."

"That's great Mrs. Johnstone, I mean Angie."

The weekend dragged. Phil already had asked a girl out for the following Saturday evening and he was counting on using some of the twenty-five dollars to buy her a burger after they made out in the car. Each day, Phil was sure that Angie would come to his apartment to tell him that she had changed her mind, that she couldn't afford to employ him after all. But she didn't.

First thing Monday morning, Phil dressed in an old pair of slacks and a slightly torn polo shirt. He knocked on Angie's door.

"Come in, Phil. The door's unlocked."

The room was in total disarray. Most of the furniture had been pushed to the center of the room and Angie was crouched in the corner, struggling with a huge sofa.

"I'm so glad you're here," she said, puffing. "Help me with this thing."

Together, they wrestled the sofa toward the middle of the room. Then they covered everything with three huge canvas drop cloths.

Working in the hot apartment, Phil soon felt sweat droplets trickle down his chest and back.

"Phil," Angie said, "you look as though you're about to die from the heat. Why don't you take off your shirt?"

"Are you sure it'd be okay?"

"Of course. We're workers, not fashion plates. After all, look at me."

Phil had been too busy to notice what Angie was wearing, but now he saw that she was dressed in a tight polo shirt and baggy, faded jeans, both covered with paint drips. As he looked at her, he realized that she had nothing on under her shirt.

He couldn't help but look at her large breasts, which swayed as she moved.

He didn't notice that Angie was watching his eyes. She moved slightly, so that her breasts jiggled, and she saw the immediate reaction in the front of Phil's tight slacks.

"Come on, Phil," she said to break the silence, "you can certainly take your shirt off. A nice-looking man like you must like to show off his body to all the girls."

Phil looked away from Angie's body and said, "If you're sure." He reached for the back of the neck of his polo shirt and pulled it off over his head.

"You have a beautiful body, Phil. You shouldn't be ashamed of it."

Phil was surprised at her reaction. No one had ever told him he had a nice-looking body.

Angie went into the kitchen and returned with a can of paint and two brushes.

"You can start on the walls and I'll work on the window frames." She snapped on a large radio and tuned it to a rock-music station. "I hope you like a little background noise. I hate the quiet myself."

They painted in silence for the rest of the morning, with only the radio for company.

It was late morning and Phil had just finished the second wall when he sensed Angie behind him. She rubbed a section of his back with a wet cloth.

"You have paint all over your back," she said. "I thought I would get you cleaned off for lunch. I hope I didn't startle you."

Phil closed his eyes as the cool cloth caressed

his back and shoulders. "No," he said lazily, "it feels just fine."

"Okay," Angie said as she backed away. "Wash up. Lunch is in ten minutes."

Ten minutes later, Phil and Angie sat in the small kitchen. They chewed on ham sandwiches and washed them down with beer. Angie made small talk, mostly about the incredibly hot weather.

"I love it when it's hot like this," Angie said as she finished her sandwich. "It makes me feel so alive."

"Yeah." Phil swigged the last of his can of beer. "Me, too." Sitting across from Angie, Phil was having a difficult time keeping his eyes off her large nipples, which showed clearly through her shirt. He ate without tasting and found it hard to concentrate on what Angie was saying.

Angie got up and cut a slice of freshly baked orange cake and set it in front of Phil. She took a bottle of cold milk from the icebox. "Beer is fine with sandwiches," she said, "but with cake, the only thing is milk." She took down a fresh glass and filled it. As she poured, she bent over so that Phil couldn't help but get a good view of her breasts down the front of her shirt.

"Good cold milk is great with cake, I always say. Isn't that right, Phil?"

"I g-g-guess so," he stammered.

"Here," Angie said as she walked around behind him, "let me show you what else a cold milk bottle is good for."

With one quick motion, she pressed the chilled bottle against the middle of Phil's overheated back.

His body stiffened and he jerked forward.

"Don't move. Let me show you." Sensuously, she slid the wet, cold bottle all over Phil's back. "Doesn't that feel wonderful?"

Phil let his head fall back. "It does feel nice," he admitted.

Still standing behind him, Angie moved the bottle to his bare chest. As she pressed its icy surface against his ribs, she moved forward so his head was pushed against the valley between her breasts. "Now, doesn't that feel good, too?"

Phil was speechless. He could feel Angie's large breasts pressing against his ears. He felt her start to sway. Her flesh stroked the sides of his head as the cold bottle stroked his chest.

"Have you ever felt anything like this before?" she purred.

"M-m-maybe we should g-g-get back to painting, Mrs. Johnstone."

"It's Angie. And we don't have to paint just yet. Isn't this more fun?" Her voice was soft and her words came out slowly.

Phil moved slightly as he tried to conceal the bulge in his pants. It was all he could do not to reach up and press Angie's breasts more firmly against the sides of his head. He took a gulp of air and tried to clear his mind.

Slowly, the bottle began to slide down his belly toward the waistband of his slacks. Angie's other hand began to slide down the wet trail.

Without moving from behind him, Angie put the bottle on the table, but she continued the sensual massage of his chest and belly. Slowly, her hand crept under the waistband of his jeans and touched the tip of his swollen penis through his white cotton underpants.

Phil was afraid to move. He was afraid that she would stop, but he was also afraid she would continue. Nothing like this had ever happened to him before and he wasn't sure that he would know what to do if it went any further. He had fucked a few girls, but always in the dark and always after he had teased and begged. And the girls always made him feel as though they had done him a favor.

Angie reached down and took his hand. She guided him to a standing position and pulled him gently into her bedroom. For the rest of his life, Phil would always remember that room: heavy mahogany furniture covered with lace doilies; a mirrored tray on the bureau with bottles of perfume and hand lotion displayed on it; lace curtains that stirred in the slight noontime breeze.

The room smelled of Jergen's lotion. Years later, he always got an erection when he smelled that particular almond aroma.

Angie guided him until he stood next to the bed. She sat on the edge of the bed, unbuckled Phil's belt, and unzipped the fly of his jeans. Ever so slowly, she pulled his pants down, until he stood in his shorts.

"Such a beautiful body," she whispered. She pressed the palm of her hand against the swelling that bulged beneath the front of his shorts. "And such a big boy, too."

He said nothing as she pulled down his shorts. He kept thinking that he should be embarrassed, but he wasn't. He was just wildly excited, afraid that if she touched him, he would shoot all over the room.

"A guy like you needs a woman like me to teach him."

"I've made it with girls before," Phil protested. He was twenty and she mustn't think he was a virgin.

"I know that," Angie said, "but you've never made love to anyone like me, have you?"

He had no time to answer, for Angie took his huge cock in her mouth and started to suck on it. It was only moments until he climaxed deep in her throat. She swallowed hard and licked her lips.

Phil was upset by how quickly he had come, but Angie said, "It's always so fast the first time I make love with someone new. Now, we have a little time." She stood up and pushed Phil to a sitting position on the bed.

Angie unbuttoned her shirt and let it fall to the floor. Then she pulled off her jeans and her underpants. "I like it when you look at me." Her body was mature but still firm. She had large breasts and a waist that had thickened over the years. Her pubic patch was large and the hair spread over much of her lower stomach.

Sensuously, she ran her hands over her skin. "Would you like to touch me and learn about how to give a woman pleasure?" She looked at Phil's penis, already erect again, and chuckled. "Of course you would."

She lay on the bed on her side next to him and rested her cheek on her palm. She took his hand and pressed it against her erect nipples. "Feel how hard they get. That's because I'm excited, anxious to feel your hard young cock inside of me."

When he moved to straddle her, she pushed him back and chuckled. "Don't rush so. Enjoy the whole experience first. Touch me all over. You want to, don't you?"

This was so different from making out in the front seat of a car. He could take his time and touch and look all he wanted.

Angie lay back. Phil ran his hands over her skin. She was moist with perspiration, so his fingers slipped and slid. She guided his fingers to the sensitive spots on her sides and her neck. Then ultimately, he touched her breasts and the insides of her thighs.

"Touch with the flats of your fingers, then with the tips. Make your touches both firm and whisper-soft like a feather. Use your fingernails to scratch lightly. Touching is a game of sensations, all kinds of sensations."

She watched his eyes and his hands as they caressed and scratched and pinched every part of her body. Slowly, his fingers ventured into her black pubic hair. "Pull some of the curls, gently. It's another sensation."

He did and he felt her gasp with pleasure. More than anything, he wanted to touch between her legs. She hadn't yet guided his hand there, but he took the initiative and slipped his hand through her hair to her hot, open flesh.

He explored every fold and smiled as she moaned. "You learn quickly," Angie said.

Remembering what she had said about sensations, he squeezed her swollen, wet outer lips gently and watched her face. Her eyes were tightly shut and the tip of her tongue flicked over her lips.

"I want to learn everything," he said hoarsely, unable to ignore the pressure building in his cock, "but I can't wait."

"It's all right. It's time for you to be inside of me now," Angie said.

They were both covered with sweat as Angie spread her legs wide and Phil placed his knees between them. His erect cock slipped into her and it took only a few strokes for him to climax.

Because of Phil's job and their frequent sexual interruptions, it took almost two weeks to finish the painting. Even when the job was completed, Phil returned to Mrs. Johnstone's apartment whenever he could and they each taught and learned.

When the summer ended and Phil's school resumed, they saw very little of each other, but when they passed on the stoop, they smiled.

Now, every summer, on the hottest day, Phil smiles and remembers.

5

EROTIC
SURROUNDINGS

Have you ever thought about making love somewhere other than the bedroom? Maybe in the bathtub, or on the dining room table? One person I know always wanted to consummate a relationship in the backseat of a stretch limousine, and another, who worked with his sexual partner, always wanted to make love on the table in the conference room.

Whatever turns you on. Just be careful that you are not interrupted, although the danger of being discovered can add to the intrigue.

Barry and Anne had always wanted to make love someplace different, someplace where they could do anything and make lots of noise doing it. This proved difficult, however, because they lived in a small apartment in a large city and had a small child. But where there's a will, there's a way.

ANNE AND BARRY'S STORY

During the two years that Anne and Barry had lived together before their marriage, they had indulged in many nights of terrific sex. Then they married and soon after Anne became pregnant. Now Mike, the baby, was just over a year old and Anne and Barry's sex life had grown stale and routine. They both knew that things should be better, but, with Barry's job and the baby, they were caught in a rut.

Barry talked about the situation with his friend Jeff one evening. "It's not that I don't love Anne," he said, "but we seem to be so tired that we fall asleep right after we put the baby down."

"I know. Carrie and I have the same problem. I never imagined that I'd be too tired for sex."

Over the next few weeks, Barry and Jeff evolved a simple plan. One Saturday, Barry and Anne kept Carrie and Jeff's three-year-old overnight so that Jeff could take Carrie to a local motel for a night away—away from their son, away from their house, away from everything that reminded them of their everyday lives.

When the young couple picked their son up late Sunday afternoon, Jeff seemed more relaxed than

Barry had seen him in months. This might be just the refresher that he and Anne needed so badly.

Barry did some planning for his night away with Anne. It was late one Saturday afternoon almost a month later when they dropped fourteen-month-old Mike off. So far, Barry hadn't confided his plans to Anne, so she sat in the passenger seat of their old car, impatiently crossing and recrossing her legs.

"Come on, Barry, give," she said finally. "Where are we going?"

"My boss and his wife are in Europe for two weeks and he's invited us to use his cabin at Sparkle Lake. It's almost a mile to the nearest neighbor. Think about it, solitude, privacy, and a swimming pool big enough to play water polo in."

Anne did think about it. She had always fantasized about making love outdoors, particularly in a swimming pool. Maybe this weekend could make that fantasy come true.

They arrived at the cabin close to sundown and, after they toured the immense house, they barbecued steaks and drank a bottle of wine Barry had brought.

It was a warm evening and the wine had added heat to their bodies, so Barry suggested, "How about a swim?"

"Do you think I could swim in my T-shirt and panties?"

"There's no one around, darling. You can swim in anything you want." He paused. "Or nothing, if you prefer."

"I think I prefer just this way," Anne said as she shed her jeans and slipped her bra off out from under her T-shirt. Her full breasts swayed as she ran toward the pool.

Barry found the control panel and turned on the soft lights, which shone from under the water. Then he turned off all the other lights and headed for the pool.

The air was soft and warm and was filled with the sounds of insects. There was a half-moon low on the horizon and the clean air allowed the light of thousands of stars to shine through.

Barry reached the pool and looked at his wife floating on her back in the center of the water. Her nipples were contracted from the cold water and, even in the dim light, he could see their shadowy outlines through the wet fabric. His eyes wandered lower and he smiled as he made out the darkened outline of Anne's pubic hair through her white nylon panties.

He pulled off his shirt and jeans and, dressed only in his briefs, dived cleanly into the water. He surfaced next to Anne, held the back of her head, and placed his wet lips on hers. The pool was seven feet deep where they bobbed, so Barry had to tread water as they kissed.

Barry pulled Anne through the cool water toward the edge of the pool, their lips still locked.

"God, you're so sexy this way," Anne said when their lips parted. She reached toward his face with her tongue and licked the water from his cheek and from the tip of his chin. Barry wrapped his arms around her and they kissed, his tongue swirling around the inside of her mouth. Anne's tongue played with Barry's, then reached inside of his mouth and felt the warmth.

Barry braced himself on the edge of the pool and lifted Anne, using the buoyancy of the water to hold her so her breasts were level with his mouth. He sucked at her erect nipples through her wet shirt. As he sucked and licked, the water from the shirt trickled into his mouth. When the shirt became drier, he let Anne's body dip into the water, then he lifted her again and continued to suck.

Anne was in heaven. She tangled her fingers in Barry's curls and held his face against her body. Every time they bobbed, the jets of cool water returning from the filter swirled between her legs, and washed over her heated skin.

After long minutes, Barry lifted Anne until she was sitting on the edge of the pool, her white panties just inches from his mouth. As she started to remove them, he stopped her. "Not yet."

Anne placed her hands behind her and leaned back and Barry stroked the wet fabric between her legs. She and Barry could feel the difference between the feel of the water and her slippery juices.

Barry, still in the water, leaned forward and sucked on the bit of white nylon between Anne's legs. He tasted chlorine mixed with Anne's special flavor. He nibbled at her clit and pulled gently at her pubic hair.

The sensations were driving Anne wild. As Barry moved, Anne alternately felt the cool of the wet material and the heat of Barry's mouth. She couldn't keep her hips still. She lifted her body, pressing her cunt harder against Barry's face.

Still licking his wife's body, Barry pulled down his briefs and threw them onto the side of the pool. He gently lifted Anne's hips and pulled her gently down into the water. As she slid down the side of the pool, he pulled the crotch of her panties aside and slid his hard cock into her hot body. Still wearing her panties and T-shirt, Anne rode on the water jets, pounding her body onto Barry's hard erection.

As water lapped against and between their bodies, Barry and Anne climaxed, almost simultaneously.

Barry crushed Anne's body between his and the side of the pool as they caught their breath. Later, Anne said, "I've always dreamed about making love in a swimming pool, but this was better than I ever imagined."

"Just wait 'til you see what I've got lined up for tomorrow," murmured Barry.

6

GAMES OF CONTROL

Before I go into the issue of control, let me say once again that it's okay to want whatever you want and it's okay to suggest new ideas and activities to your partner.

With this in mind, read on with an open mind and a sense of adventure.

Control. Many people want to have sexual control taken from their hands. Women often express this through rape fantasies, dreams in which a handsome man ravishes a woman's body without her consent. I freely admit that I am one of those women. It is vitally important, however, that everyone understand that the kind of rape I fantasize about has nothing to do with actual rape. Actual rape is a brutal physical assault, intercourse without consent. That idea is repugnant.

The rape I fantasize about merely involves the total loss of control. I love the idea that I am no longer responsible for my own pleasure, or lack thereof. I am no longer responsible for my partner's pleasure, either. I just do as I'm told, or I am completely passive while I am ravished.

For me, a particularly delicious thought that helps to remove control completely is: Don't climax until I've given you permission. Then, I'm no longer expected to perform. (Yes, women do have performance anxiety, too.)

There are also those who want to assume control, to have someone "at their mercy." Either a man or a woman may want to be able to demand the kind of sexual activity that they've always wanted—a long period of oral sex, or a particular sexual position, for example.

If you and your partner are on opposite sides, one dominant and one submissive, that's wonderful. Go for it. Try bondage or a master-slave relationship for an evening, but always remember to listen for your partner to "holler uncle." (See page 97.)

If you discover that you are both on the same side, try alternating roles. You may discover that the pleasure you get from pleasing your partner as she has never been pleasured before will make up for your being in a less comfortable role. Also, you may be able to give him ideas for the next time when the roles are reversed.

You could also pretend, via a story, that you are both being controlled by a third party who makes you do things to each other while he watches. In the last chapter of the book, "Story Starters," there is one called "Control." (See page 218.) Try acting it out. There are many tantalizing diversions possible.

Control takes on many forms. The control doesn't have to be real or be expressed by force. Brian found that out one evening.

BRIAN'S STORY

Franz Anton Mesmer: Brian knew all about him— born 1734, died 1815. He was the founder of what he called "animal magnetism," now known as hypnosis.

Brian had been fascinated by mesmerism since, as a youngster, he had dreamed of giving shows and amazing all his friends. He would imagine himself performing before huge audiences. Everyone would ooh and aah about the wondrous things that he could get people to do under hypnosis. He even studied the technique, but he never actually got anyone to agree to be hypnotized.

As a young adult, his fantasies took on a new form. There was no audience, only Brian and a beautiful girl who was completely under his power. Late into the evening, he would fantasize about what he would have this girl do. Many a night, he lay in bed and stroked himself while taking his fantasy to the limits of his imagination.

After he met Janet, his fantasy life became less active. They married and their sex life was wonderful, full and rich.

It had been years since he had last thought of animal magnetism, but when his son Craig came to him and asked for suggestions for a fifth-grade biography, Brian remembered his own fascination with Mesmer. After several long discussions, Craig decided to do his biography on Mesmer and Brian began to revisit some of his old fantasies.

One evening, after a long discussion about the eighteenth-century hypnotist, Craig wandered off to bed and left Brian and Janet in the living room.

"You really got into that mesmerization stuff, didn't you?" Janet said.

"Sure did," Brian answered, shifting to relieve the ache in his groin that occurred every time he thought about hypnosis.

"I've always been interested in what it must be like to be completely in someone's power," Janet wondered aloud.

Brian couldn't believe his ears. Not wanting to jump to conclusions, Brian merely said, "In what way?"

"Well," Janet continued, "it sounds kinky, I mean having someone order you around. You wouldn't have to think whether it was all right to do something. You would have no choice. You would just do as you were told." She blushed and looked very embarrassed by what she had just said. "I guess that's pretty silly."

Brian tried to swallow the lump in his throat.

Casually, he said, "I used to be able to hypnotize people." It was only a small lie, he reasoned. He had almost done it once.

Janet's eyes got round. "Really? I always wanted to be hypnotized. Could we try sometime?"

"Maybe," Brian said. "We would need complete privacy and quiet. Distractions are bad."

Janet would not be put off. "Craig is spending the weekend with Joey. How about Friday night?"

Brian had a hard time believing what he heard. "Sure, I guess," he said. Stay calm Brian, he said to himself.

The rest of the week, he wondered whether he could really do it. He went to the public library on his lunch hour and spent every afternoon reading and trying to remember everything he had ever learned.

Friday evening, Janet, Brian, and Craig had dinner and then Janet drove Craig to his friend's house for the weekend. In the silence of the house, Brian continued to read and hoped that he wouldn't look like an idiot in front of his wife.

As he heard Janet open the front door, he quickly hid the book. Whatever he knew would have to do.

"Okay," Janet said without preamble. "Are we really going to try it?"

"If you're sure. But I don't know whether it will work. Some people are more difficult to hypnotize than others."

"I bet I'll make a great subject. What do I have to do?"

Brian dimmed the lights and had his wife sit in a comfortable chair. He wanted this to work so badly, but he was also nervous, afraid of making a fool of himself. He had bought a cheap crystal pendant, which he used for Janet to focus on. His hand shook so much that he had a hard time keeping the pendant swinging smoothly.

For five long minutes, he did everything he could remember to put her into a trance. Brian kept wanting to test whether it had worked, but he was afraid.

Finally, he looked at her carefully. Janet's eyes were closed and her face and hands appeared completely relaxed. "From now on, you will do exactly as I tell you. You will concentrate on my voice and respond only to it."

It was time to test the depth of her trance. "Raise your right hand," he said to her.

He held his breath. Ever so slowly, her right hand rose.

"Put it down on your knee," he said, and her hand moved to her knee. He couldn't believe it. It had actually worked.

Now for some harder things, he thought. He had her stand, then sit. He had her sing a nursery rhyme and bark like a dog. It all seemed to work. He decided to try to waken her, then have her return to her trance when he snapped his fingers. That worked, too.

Could it really be true? Did he really have his wife completely in his power?

"Unbutton your blouse," he commanded. Slowly,

she unbuttoned her blouse. "Now, take it off." She did.

Janet sat with her eyes closed, her breathing gentle. Her chest rose and fell under her white cotton bra. It was driving Brian crazy. She was really his to do with what he liked.

"Take your bra off, too." She unhooked the bra and pulled the straps down. Then she dropped it onto the floor next to her shirt.

Brian gazed at her breasts. He had always loved her body. "Hold your tits for me," he said. Janet slid her hands under her flesh and held her breasts out for him.

Brian leaned forward and opened his mouth. "Put your nipple in my mouth. I want to suck on it."

Eyes still closed, Janet leaned forward and grazed her nipple over his cheek toward his mouth. He sucked and heard the loud noises he made. He always had been afraid that sounds would turn his wife off, but now he could do as he liked and tell her to forget everything when she awoke. He could also make Janet do exactly what he wanted, too.

When he had sucked enough, he said, "I want you to remove the rest of your clothes. But you must do it very slowly, like a stripper would."

Still in a trance, Janet began to move her hips seductively as she pulled down the zipper on her jeans. Brian sat back against the sofa cushions and watched. Ever so slowly, Janet lowered her jeans and then her underpants. Naked, she danced and swayed to some music that only she could hear.

"You can open your eyes now," he said. Slowly, Janet's eyes opened and she gazed blankly at him.

Brian started to unbutton his shirt, but then he reconsidered. "Come here," he said, "and unbutton my shirt."

Her face bland, Janet walked over to the couch. One at a time, she worked each button through its buttonhole.

"Now, pull it off."

Under Brian's instructions, Janet undressed him completely. As she removed his shorts, her hands brushed his erection. He gasped and wondered how he could last long enough to do all the things he wanted to do.

To give himself time to calm down, he said, "Close your eyes and lie down here." He patted the sofa beside him and Janet lay down with her head on the arm.

"Listen to me and understand. You're alone in bed and you're very excited. You need to relieve the hunger that's making your body so hot. Now, spread your legs and touch yourself. It's the only way to satisfy your terrible hunger." He felt a little silly saying those things, but when he saw Janet's hand slowly move between her legs, he stopped caring how he sounded.

"So hungry, yes," she murmured.

Expertly, Janet's fingers began to stroke her clitoris.

"That's right," he said. "You're still so hungry and the hunger is increasing as your fingers explore your body. Your nipples are hard and erect. Your hunger is there, too. Touch your breast with one hand and your pussy with the other. It's the only way to ease your suffering."

From where he sat near her feet, he could watch her hands as she gave herself pleasure. Suddenly, instead of wanting to fuck her, Brian wanted to watch her face as she climaxed. "You can feel the orgasm building inside of you. You cannot control the excitement. You're going to come, aren't you?"

"Yes," she whispered.

"That's wonderful. I want you to climax. I want to see you come."

Suddenly, her back arched and her mouth opened. She threw her head back and a cry of pleasure burst from her lips. Her hands kept stroking and fondling until the ripples of pleasure stopped.

While he waited for Janet's breathing to ease, he debated with himself. He knew exactly what he wanted, what had haunted his fantasies for so many years, but he was still hesitant.

Janet lay quietly with her eyes closed. "Janet," he said, "you're still hungry, but not in your pussy. The hunger's all in your hands and your mouth. Your hand aches with the need to touch me. The only thing you can think about to relieve your hunger is my cock. You want to hold it and suck it."

"Yes," she whispered, "hold you and suck you." Her eyes opened and she gazed at Brian's cock. "Let me hold you."

"I want you to touch me. Do whatever you need to ease your hunger."

Hesitantly, Janet got up and knelt between Brian's legs. She reached out and touched Brian's cock, which was huge and stood up in front of his belly. The tip glistened with tiny drops of fluid.

She wrapped her hand around his cock and squeezed. She stroked and fondled his balls. She flicked the tip of her tongue over the end of his penis. Still stroking the base, she took the end of his erection in her mouth and tasted the salty fluid.

With increasing enthusiasm, she sucked and stroked until Brian knew he couldn't hold back any longer. He knew that Janet usually didn't like him to climax in her mouth, but he would tell her to forget. He reached down and placed one hand on the back of her head and one hand on her throat. He wanted to feel her swallow his come.

He climaxed deep in her throat. Over and over, he spurted. He could feel the movements in her neck as she swallowed. He couldn't remember having been so excited or so satisfied.

Heavily, he let his head fall back onto the sofa cushions as Janet sat quietly on the floor between his legs. He knew that he would have to waken her soon and be sure that she forgot what she had just done, but he wanted to float here a bit longer.

As his mind cleared, he panicked. How would he explain what had just happened? He would have to tell Janet something. She would know from the wetness that remained from her orgasm and maybe from the taste in her mouth. He couldn't tell her what he had done, it was just too weird. She would be shocked.

He took a deep breath and let it out. "It was so wonderful," he whispered.

"It certainly was," Janet said.

It took a moment for the words to register. Janet shouldn't be saying anything. He jerked his head up and looked at her as she gazed up at him. "What did you say?" he asked.

Slowly, a huge grin spread over her face. "I said that it certainly was wonderful."

"You're not hypnotized!" he said.

"I won't tell if you won't." She giggled. Then she climbed onto the sofa and wrapped her arms around Brian's chest.

"I don't understand," Brian said.

"I enjoyed tonight more than I've enjoyed anything for a long time. Don't try to understand why I love being completely under your control, darling. Just accept that I love it when you tell me what to do. I don't have to be afraid of doing things wrong. I know I'm doing exactly what you want me to."

Brian said nothing. He stared at Janet and tried to understand what she was saying.

"I've always wanted to do the things we did tonight," Janet continued, "but I was afraid. This hypnotism thing seemed to give me the opportunity to belong to you completely. And it was just as erotic as I imagined it would be."

She looked into Brian's eyes. "Are you disappointed that I wasn't really hypnotized? Isn't it enough that I was under your spell and that we both enjoyed it?"

"You really enjoyed it?"

"More than I ever thought I would."

"I did, too," Brian admitted. "Your hands and your mouth drove me crazy. It was really all right that I watched you come?"

Janet hugged him tightly. "Stop worrying. Just promise me that you'll mesmerize me again soon."

Brian smiled and nodded. He wrapped his arms around his wife and thought about all the things he would have her do the next time she was "under his power."

Bondage. Bondage is a way to establish a different type of control. Obviously, someone who is tied up cannot have any say in what's happening and the partner is completely free to do anything. It's control, however, not force. Bondage is never meant to be a way to *force* someone to cooperate. All these games are for two partners who both enjoy the activity.

If you decide to try tying someone up, use whatever is handy. It's not necessary to begin with "The Beginners Bondage Kit," purchased from a catalog. Later on, however, reminding your partner that you own restraints and intend to use them may be enough to start your juices flowing.

Old neckties, stockings, soft ribbon, or rope make ideal restraints. Don't use wire or thin twine that will cut into flesh, and take extreme care not to tie so tightly that you cause injury. In the heat of passion, you might not notice that bonds have become too tight. You or your partner could end up with marks that are difficult to explain or even painful. Be careful of burns as you slide rope around your partner's body. Also, use bow- or slipknots that can be untied quickly in emergency situations, but don't tie your partner in such a way that he can get free. Nothing ruins a bondage fantasy more quickly than being tied and knowing you can get out. It defeats the whole purpose. And definitely let your partner "suffer" by watching you tie him up. Tell him what you're doing as you bind him very slowly and then list the things you're going to do later. It's incredibly arousing.

Also, don't restrict yourself to tying your partner spread-eagled to the bed. Try facedown, or face-up, with wrists tied to ankles or knees. Try tying her hands behind her back, or tying her up on her hands and knees. Tie him bent over a table, with wrists and ankles tied to the legs, or over the back of a chair. The varieties are endless. Some are described in the sections that follow. Others, you'll have the pleasure of discovering on your own.

Hollering Uncle. One of the enjoyable parts of role playing and bondage is being able to yell for help, scream, or beg for mercy. On the other hand, it is vital for the one in control to know when she has gone so far that the excitement level is being reduced, not heightened. These games are not supposed to be one-sided. They are supposed to provide pleasure to both parties. When this is no longer true, it's time to stop.

Therefore, it is most important that you have a

code word, agreed to in advance, that means, "I really want you to stop." My partner and I use the term *holler uncle.* This allows us to get as deeply into acting out a fantasy as we wish without any misunderstandings.

These control games are not supposed to be endurance contests. Don't wait so long to holler uncle that all the pleasure is gone. I have done that on occasion, afraid to spoil the enjoyment for my partner, and I have ended up spoiling an enjoyable experience for both of us.

Sometimes the opportunity for a new control game appears where you least expect it. If you have your mind open, you will realize what your partner is suggesting and you can seize the moment. As you will see in the story that follows, Susan and Frank explored their game of control after an evening of role playing and dressing up. Before we get to their story, however, let's take a moment to talk about playing dress-up, an activity that can lead to many interesting new places.

Playing Dress-up. I have played dress-up many times, but I'll never forget the first time. I felt so silly, I almost chickened out. For Valentine's Day, my partner had given me a tiny red G-string with a zipper up the skimpy front and a bikini top with zippers up each bra cup, and I wanted to put it on that evening. While my partner was in the bathroom, I undressed and stared at the small bits of fabric. I swallowed hard and put the two pieces on. As I stood and looked at myself in the mirror over my bureau, I felt ridiculous. I was then in my mid-forties, with a decent, but not twenty-year-old figure. I had a few bulges in places that were no longer hidden. It also felt aggressive, as if I was inviting sex, which nice girls didn't do.

I started to pull the top off when I heard the bathroom door open behind me. My eyes were drawn to my partner's face as he looked at me. In that moment, all my embarrassment disappeared. The look on his face made it all worthwhile.

Needless to say, playing dress-up is very awkward the first time, particularly for a woman. Women, throughout their lives, have been brainwashed into believing that they are supposed to be passive and not the ones to initiate sexual activity. Dressing up in costume is unfamiliar and somehow sexually aggressive, at least for me.

It's also exciting, however, especially if your partner is turned on by particular clothing. Remember that a few seductive clothes are more alluring than no clothes at all. Peruse some of those lingerie catalogs. Try a teddy, or a lacy slip or nightgown. Wear one of those bras with half cups or crotchless panties. Tell him what you're wearing under your clothes before you go out for an evening and then let anticipation heighten the experience.

There is also something extraerotic about making love almost fully dressed. My partner loves to reach under my skirt, knowing that I am naked underneath. Try going without underpants or bra and then make love on the kitchen counter or in the yard while still mostly dressed.

Go through your wardrobe and find some items that you no longer want. Then consider them disposable clothing and let your partner know that you'd like to have your clothing ripped or slowly cut off of your body, maybe while you're tied up.

If you aren't in the mood for dressing up in unusual clothing, buy some different makeup or wild costume jewelry for you or your partner. If it's for you, use it to change your looks for a particular game. A change in your looks can frequently bring about a change in your behavior and that of your partner. If the new article is for your partner, package it with a copy of an erotic story or wrap it in a relevant article from a magazine to suggest the roles you'd like to play. If you've gotten into dominant/submissive games, wear appropriate clothes—black pants and top, leather, or something lacy and feminine. Try dressing up as a student and teacher or sultan and slave or doctor and patient. The possibilities are endless. Dressing up can change your whole outlook.

SUSAN AND FRANK'S STORY

Susan decided later that the Halloween party changed her life. "Changed her life" sounded like an overstatement, but after that evening, her relationship with her husband, Frank, was not the same.

When they married seven years earlier, Frank was a construction worker. The Southern California sun bronzed his six-foot-two-inch, 180-pound body and lightened his sandy blond hair. The hard physical labor toughened his body so not a bit of fat remained. His blue eyes sparkled and he had an infectious smile. Now he was a foreman, but he still worked outdoors most of the time.

Susan worked as a secretary for four lawyers and frequently lamented her work load and late nights. She hated the fact that she had to wear conservative business suits that effectively concealed the soft curves of her five-foot-three-inch body. She kept her brown eyes hidden beneath large tortoiseshell glasses and she wore little makeup.

The change in their lives began when their friends Tom and Jennifer invited them to a Halloween masquerade party. Frank and Susan discussed their costumes at length and quickly discarded the standard period outfits. They both wanted something much more creative, something that would allow each of them to be a bit exhibitionistic. Their costumes would be a complete change from their five-day-a-week nine-to-five existence. It was the day before the party when they hit upon the idea. Susan would play a girl pirate and Frank would be her slave and bodyguard. They rushed around to a number of costume shops and rummaged deep into their closets until they finally put together the exact outfits they wanted.

The evening of the party, to heighten their grand entrance, they arrived late, both wearing trench coats.

First, Susan dramatically removed her coat. Conversation stopped as her costume was revealed. She wore black short shorts, which barely covered her behind, and a bright red shirt, which she had unbuttoned to reveal a good amount of cleavage. Over the shirt, she wore a black bolero jacket, and the lower half of her long legs was encased in tall black boots polished to a high shine. She had covered her eyes with a small black domino mask.

After Susan removed her coat, she put on a large black pirate hat and buckled a sword around her hips. Then, with great ceremony, she snapped her fingers.

"Yes, ma'am," Frank said. Then he removed his coat. He was wearing tight black pants with a pair of black boots. The only other thing he wore was a black leather slave collar.

The women at the party stared at his heavily

muscled chest, which he had lightly oiled. He looked as if he could crush someone with his huge fists and heavily knotted forearms. The guests couldn't quite see his face because, although he towered over Susan, he kept his head lowered submissively. Slowly, Susan opened the paper bag she was carrying and removed the last part of her costume, a heavy black whip with a wicked-looking black leather handle.

Susan used the handle of the whip to raise Frank's unmasked face. "He's not masked," Susan explained to their hostess. "Slaves may not cover their faces."

Jennifer giggled and stared at Frank's body.

"Hang these coats, slave," Susan said, trailing the whip along the floor as she walked.

"Yes, ma'am," Frank responded.

When Frank returned, Susan spoke to him loudly enough for everyone to hear. "Get me a drink. And make sure it has enough ice."

When Frank returned, there was no ice in Susan's drink. "I told you to put enough ice in this, slave," she snapped.

"I'm sorry. I'll get you another one. Just please, don't whip me later," he begged, much to the amusement of the crowd that had gathered around Susan.

"As long as you behave and don't give me any more trouble," Susan said.

Frank spent the evening serving Susan and enjoying it. And Susan loved the control she had over him.

At midnight, Susan unmasked and their host announced the prizewinners. To no one's surprise, Frank and Susan won first prize, but the best prize for both of them came a little later.

On the trip home, Frank was strangely silent. He was absorbed in thoughts of the evening. He had had a wonderful time. He had served Susan, fetching and carrying. A few times, she had ordered him to dance with the women at the party. He had obeyed without question and had regretted the time he had to spend with the weak, ineffectual women. When he was not actually serving her, Frank stood and waited for Susan to give him something to do to make her happy. He didn't have to think.

All day I give orders, he thought now. I have to be tough and never relax for a moment. It's so good to be able to just follow orders, not to have to worry about what decision to make and about the thousand ramifications.

He also found himself sexually aroused all evening. He had had to rearrange his clothing several times to make room for his large erection. He wasn't sure why he was so excited, and he didn't care. He just wanted it to continue.

They arrived home and Frank hung up Susan's coat. Then he stood in front of her with his head down and handed her the whip. Please let her understand, he prayed.

Very softly, he said, "Don't whip me, ma'am. I'll serve you in any way you want."

Susan looked at her husband. She also had

enjoyed the roles they had played that evening. No longer did she have to take orders and be the dutiful servant. She had been the master and Frank had done anything she wanted. She had even ordered him to dance with a woman whom she knew he detested and he had followed her instructions without a question.

She looked at his subservient posture and tried to read his body language. Could he really mean what she thought he did? She glanced at the front of his trousers, saw the obvious bulge, and smiled. She had had a few drinks and she was willing to take a little risk. She would see what happened.

She used the whip handle to raise his face. "Look at me," she said. It was all there in his eyes. "You're still my slave, aren't you?" she asked sternly.

Frank nodded.

"When I ask you a question, I want to hear your answer."

"Yes, ma'am," he said.

"Get me a drink. Lots of ice."

While Frank was in the kitchen, Susan walked over to the sofa and sat down. She crossed her long legs and waited.

Frank returned with Susan's drink, this time with plenty of ice. He leaned down and handed it to her.

"Kneel down," she said.

Frank got down on his knees. "Remove my boots," Susan said.

As he pulled off her boots, he ran his hand down the inside of her thighs.

"Do you want a whipping?" Susan snapped. "You are not to touch me unless I tell you to."

"I'm sorry, ma'am. I won't let it happen again."

"And by the way," Susan said, "I see that bulge in your pants. It is mine. You may not touch it and you better not climax unless I allow it. Is that understood?"

Frank lowered his head to hide his smile. "Yes, ma'am," he murmured.

Susan thought for a moment. "I think I'd like a bath." It was past 1:00 A.M., but she wasn't at all tired.

"I'll run it for you."

Frank called Susan fifteen minutes later. He had filled the tub and added some of Susan's favorite bath salts.

"It's just the right temperature," he said.

Susan stood in the middle of the bathroom. "Undress me," she ordered. "But don't touch. If I want to be touched, I'll tell you where."

Frank gently removed Susan's jacket and unbuttoned her blouse. Twice his fingers grazed her skin and she glared at him.

"You touched me," she said. "If that happens again, I will use my whip. You have to learn discipline."

Frank kept his head lowered and said nothing.

Susan ran her hands under her large breasts, raising them for Frank to see. "Would you like to touch these?" she asked.

"Oh, yes, ma'am."

"Then touch. Gently!"

His hands brushed over the tips of Susan's erect nipples. Then he softly kneaded her flesh and swirled his fingertips toward the center.

"Suck my tits, slave," Susan said.

Frank bent down until his mouth was level with her breasts. He took one nipple in his mouth and sucked it. When he felt that it was as hard as it could get, he switched his mouth to the other one and sucked it reverently.

"That's enough," Susan said as she pressed Frank down onto his haunches. "I want my bath now."

Frank pulled her shorts and underpants down. He wanted to touch her. He wanted to throw her down on the floor and fuck her senseless, but he couldn't. She wouldn't like it and she might punish him.

Susan stepped into the tub and sank down into the warm water. She was glad that she had stopped him. She might have climaxed right there, just from the feeling of his mouth.

"Wash me," she said.

Frank took a facecloth and rubbed the bar of soap across it. Then he slowly rubbed the cloth all over Susan's body. As he washed the insides of her thighs, he waited for her to stop him, but she didn't, so he began to stroke her between her legs. Slowly, he rubbed the cloth through the water, back and forth over her sweet cunt.

"Enough," she said as she grabbed his wrist. "I'm ready to get out."

While she rinsed off the soap, Frank got a big bath towel. Susan stepped out and Frank rubbed her all over with the towel. When she was dry, they walked into the bedroom.

"Take off your pants. I want to see exactly what my slave has underneath."

Frank pulled his pants down as Susan stretched out on the bed.

He was enormous, larger than she had ever seen him. "Now touch yourself," she said, "but don't come."

Frank looked at Susan. Her eyes were bright with passion and her mouth was slightly open. He had never touched his penis with anyone watching, but he had no choice. She had ordered him to.

He wrapped his hand around his erection and ran it over the length of his cock. "I'm afraid I'll displease you, ma'am. If I do this any longer, I'll climax."

"Do as you're told. And don't you dare come. There will be serious consequences if you climax without permission." She left him no choice. He had to do as she commanded. As he stroked his cock, he let his head fall back and closed his eyes. Sweat started to bead on his forehead.

It took all his concentration to keep from climaxing, but he continued to stroke himself slowly while Susan watched. He dug his fingernails into his palm to keep from coming.

Just as he was about to lose control, she stopped him with a loud slap across his ass. "I want your mouth between my legs."

Frank obeyed quickly. He crawled to the foot of the bed and then up between Susan's legs.

His tongue was for her pleasure only. He used it like an instrument to stroke her cunt, first slowly, then with short, quick strokes. Her juices were flowing freely and, as he varied his licks, he felt her body respond. He was unreasonably glad that he was able to give his mistress pleasure.

His mistress. Yes, he thought, it felt right. He was made to serve her.

"You may fuck me now, if you like," she said.

"What I want is unimportant. I would love to fuck you, but only if it's what you want. I want only to please you."

He looked up at her face. She was smiling. "That's the right answer. And I want you right now," she said.

Quickly, he crawled up and slid his cock into her. He watched her and adjusted his movements as he gauged her level of arousal. Yes, he said to himself, she's ready.

As he thrust into her as hard as he could, he reached down and rubbed her clit. He was rewarded by the feel of her climax.

"Now!" she screamed. "Come now!"

He came, flooding her with his semen. His orgasm seemed to last forever.

When they were finally still, he asked, "May I hold you?"

She smiled as he enfolded her in his arms. It was like some fairy tale. Neither of them understood what had happened or where their relationship would go from here. They knew only that they had found something intensely pleasurable that they could share for as long as they wanted.

○ ● ○

Susan and Frank discovered that a way to enhance their sex lives was to change who was in control of their sexual activities.

If you are the leader of a game of control, open your mind and express your desires freely. That's what your submissive partner wants you to do. Tell him where to touch or squeeze or lick. Tell him what kind of strokes you want.

If you are following a leader, make mental notes of what she is asking for, then incorporate them into your lovemaking at other times. Remember that she is giving you ideas for the future.

And there are so many more ideas left to explore. . .

7

TOYS

It is said that you can tell the men from the boys by the kind of toys they play with . . .

Toys are wonderful but they pose some problems, such as how to buy them. I live near New York City and have access to a few "adult only" stores. It's a mixed blessing. It's wonderful to have all the toys displayed and available, but I find that going into one of *those* stores is still very embarrassing.

I have to admit that my partner was the first of us to visit an "adult only" store. While I was running an errand in the neighborhood, he wandered inside and, with amazing aplomb, bought a dildo. When we met later, he brandished a brown paper bag and told me what he had done. I complimented him on his bravery. That evening, he used our new toy to drive me crazy.

Weeks later, at his urging, we made our first trip to that same "adult only" store together to buy a vibrator. I was then forty-six years old and I had never owned one. He convinced me that the only way to decide what kind we wanted was to go there and explore.

The afternoon we visited, the store was empty except for the two of us and a salesman. I was amazed. The room was filled with everything from love oil to adult books, from outrageously funny greeting cards to dildos in every color and size. I blushed as I spotted the dildo he had bought on his first trip there.

Although at least fifteen different kinds of vibrators were displayed, they were all behind the counter. I realized that one of us would have to ask to see them, since neither of us knew anything about them. Thank heavens, my partner was amazingly suave about the whole thing. He asked the young man behind the counter if we could see a few different ones.

Almost immediately, a woman appeared from the back of the store and she and the salesman began to ask us questions and give us advice.

"Is this for use alone or for using together? Different types serve different purposes."

"Have you any experience with vibrators?"

"Remember not to leave it on for more than twenty minutes."

"Do you want one that is battery-operated or will you have an outlet handy? Battery-operated vibrators give you more freedom, but have less power."

I think that business was slow and they just

wanted to relieve their boredom, but I thought I would sink into the floor. As I turned away and pretended to be interested in some placebo tablets to increase sexual potency, my partner made a thorough study, then selected and bought a vibrator. We hustled out and only then did he admit that he had been as nervous as I. Embarrassed or not, we had our vibrator and we still have it and use it today.

You can also buy toys by mail. There are usually ads in most sex magazines with illustrations and graphic descriptions of everything from leather restraints and handcuffs to penis-shaped water pistols and watches that state "Time for Sex." Some of the items will disappoint; some will live up to every expectation.

LINDA'S STORY

Linda and Rick had been bookmarking for about six months. They had gotten over their initial embarrassment quickly and could now admit to and discuss fantasies that they wanted to play out. They also had made arrangements with a neighbor to trade off their children. One weekend, they had Patsy and Don's twins; another weekend, their three boys stayed next door.

One day when Rick was not coming home until late, Linda found an issue of an erotic magazine beside her bed. In it, she found a bookmark. Curious to find out what Rick was interested in now, she opened the magazine.

The bookmark was inserted in a two-page spread advertising dildos, vibrators, and other sex toys.

Many women she knew were open about owning and using a vibrator. There was even a line about being grown up and owning your own vibrator in the movie *An Unmarried Woman,* which she had seen four times.

But could she really buy something like that? Could she really call some 800 number and order a dildo or vibrator as if she was ordering a new pair of slacks?

She stared at the advertisement for a long time. She had no idea whether she wanted to order anything at all, but the fact that Rick had bookmarked it for her made her consider the idea. She knew that she wasn't interested in paddles or latex whips and she quickly bypassed ball gags and restraints. She didn't think she was ready for any of that—at least not yet.

Her gaze kept returning to an ad for a penis-shaped vibrator. "Orgasm guaranteed," it said. Next to it was a picture of a dildo. "Life-size, flesh-colored—once she uses it, she'll beg for it," the ad stated.

The next afternoon, Linda gathered her courage, got the magazine, pulled out her credit card, and dialed the 800 number. She stammered through giving the operator her credit card number and the code numbers next to the items she had selected, the vibrator and the dildo. All the time, she was thinking, Thank God I don't have to describe what I'm ordering. When she was finished, the operator assured her that her order would be delivered within four weeks, in a plain wrapper.

All she had to do was wait.

She put the magazine back on Rick's nightstand. That night, although he said nothing, Linda knew that Rick was aware the magazine had been re-turned.

Several weeks later the box arrived. Linda hid it in her closet until the following Friday evening. Just before she was to escort the children to their neighbor's house for the night, she slipped upstairs and put the untouched box, still in its original plain brown wrapping, on Rick's side of the bed. Still saying nothing, she hustled the children out and walked them next door.

"Linda," Rick called as he heard her return, "I'm in the living room. Come in here as soon as you put your coat away." His voice sounded so casual. Maybe he hasn't seen the box yet, she thought.

"Okay," she answered. "Be right in."

When she entered the living room, Rick was sitting with the contents of the box spread out in front of him on the coffee table. Linda's blush made her feel hot all over.

"It makes you uncomfortable, doesn't it?" Rick said softly.

Linda nodded.

"Is that bad," Rick continued, "or does it also heighten the anticipation for you as much as it does for me?"

"Are you embarrassed, too?" Linda asked, her eyes wide.

"Of course," he said, "but I'm also wildly excited. I was hoping you'd order some things like these. I would have ordered some toys for us myself, but I wasn't really sure you'd be interested."

"I wasn't, either, but the fact that you invited me to pick something—"

"Come over here," Rick interrupted.

Linda recognized the heavy-lidded look in Rick's eyes. The fact that they were not in the bedroom didn't surprise her. When they had the luxury of privacy, they often made love in the living room.

Linda crossed the room and sat next to Rick. "Don't think about anything," he said. "I'm new at this, too, so just say stop if I do something that hurts you or that you don't like."

Linda nodded again and tried to relax as Rick's arms went around her and he pushed her back against the arm of the couch. His lips were warm and soft on hers as he kissed her. He took a long time pressing his mouth against hers, teasing her tongue with his. His hands were working the tightness from the backs of her shoulders and the length of his body was pressing against her.

Gradually, she started to relax. She could feel some of the fear and tension dissipate. Rick was an expert at touching Linda's body.

Slowly, his mouth began the slow trip down the side of her neck. He licked and nibbled until he reached the erotic spot where her shoulder joined her neck. He swirled his tongue, then blew on the wet area. Shivers rippled up and down Linda's back.

He slid his hands around and fondled her full breasts, seeking her nipples through her blouse and bra. Linda's breasts had always been particularly sensitive and this time was no different. As he alternately pinched and stroked, Linda made soft moaning sounds deep in her throat. Her arms wrapped around him, cupped his buttocks, and pressed his erect penis against her belly.

One button at a time, Rick undid Linda's blouse. He reached behind her and unhooked her bra. Without touching her naked flesh, he pulled her clothes aside. Then he did what always had driven his wife crazy. He pursed his lips and blew a stream of cold air across her nipples.

She gasped as the flesh contracted and her nipples formed tiny points.

"Do you want me to suck your tits?" he asked in a throaty voice.

"Yes," she groaned. "Please."

He leaned over, but instead of sucking at her erect nipples, he used the tip of his tongue to circle the area of darkened flesh around one. Then he blew on the wetness, causing Linda to suck in a gulp of air and raise her chest.

"Anxious, aren't you?" Rick said.

"Please," she answered. "I want your mouth on me."

Linda's talk always excited Rick, partly because it was still hard for her to use the explicit language they loved.

"You want my mouth on what?" he said.

"You know," she said.

"Tell me," he said.

"My nipples," she said slowly.

"You mean your tits?"

"Yes."

"Say it!"

Linda shuddered. "Suck my tits."

Rick quickly obliged. He buried his face in her soft flesh, enjoying the scent and the taste of her. He drew a nipple into his mouth and flicked the tip with his tongue. Linda was straining her entire body, trying to get closer to him.

He sucked each nipple in turn until he knew she wanted him desperately. He quickly pulled off their clothes, and then they lay together naked. Rick suspected that Linda, in her lust, had forgotten about the new toys.

Rick returned to Linda's breasts until her hips were thrashing against the cushions.

"You want my hard cock inside of you?" he asked.

"Yes," she answered.

"Maybe this big cock will feel better."

Linda's eyes flew open as she suddenly remembered the toys. She didn't have any time to react, however, since Rick had the large dildo in his hand

and started to stroke her slippery, hot clit with the cool plastic.

"This won't hurt a bit," Rick said, using a line from their favorite "playing doctor" fantasy.

Firmly, he pressed the dildo against the opening to her vagina. She was so open and wet that it slid in easily.

Rick had a rather large penis, but this dildo was oversized. It stretched Linda's skin as it slid in and out and the cold added an unfamiliar yet exciting aspect.

"Oh God," she said, "it feels so good inside me." Her hips bucked and pressed up against the invasion. Rick fucked Linda with the large dildo, first with fast, hard strokes, then with slow, smooth, teasing ones. Then he pulled it out and reinserted just the tip. He used short strokes to push it in only a short way, then he pulled it out again.

Linda was going crazy. "I am going to come," she cried, "but I want your hard cock inside of me when I do."

Quickly, Rick withdrew the dildo and pulled Linda down onto the thick carpet. He climbed on top of her and pushed his erect penis into her as far as it would go. It took only a few thrusts for both of them to climax.

A moment later, panting, Linda said, "That was wonderful. I've never felt anything like it."

Suddenly, Linda was afraid that Rick would think that the dildo was a substitute for his body. "It doesn't mean that I will settle for only that thing."

Rick smiled. "I know that. But it does make you

hot, doesn't it? I hoped it would, because it makes me so horny watching that dildo slide in and out of your pussy."

"It made me hungry in a way I never expected. I think you don't have to be a mind reader to figure that out."

"Have you any idea how much it excited me to see you so excited?" Rick said. "I watched your body thrash around as I fucked you with that dildo and I thought I would come right then."

"Really?" Linda said. "It's really okay that I enjoyed that?"

Rick grinned wickedly. "And you realize that we haven't even taken the vibrator out of the plastic wrapper yet."

8

MASSAGE

There are many types of massage. Therapeutic massage takes years to master. In many states, hundreds of hours of study are needed and strict licensing requirements must be met before one can call oneself a massage therapist. I've had this type of massage and it's wonderful. Nothing refreshes you in quite the same way. It can also ease sore muscles and relax overstressed brains.

Another type, sexual massage, has gotten a bad reputation over the years. Massage parlors are usually dingy places where some man or woman will give you any type of massage you want. Often, *massage parlor* is just a euphemism for a house of prostitution.

Massage need be neither of these. It can be a mutually enjoyable experience consisting of touching and exploring. Simple nonsexual techniques can be learned through adult-education programs. Many colleges have such courses. Take one if you wish or buy one of the many books available on the subject. There are also videotapes that teach massage techniques. Any of these will help you learn where to begin and will show you a few basic principles. However, whether or not you have mastered any technique, the fun part is practicing on your partner. Then let your mind wander into the realm of erotic massage. You don't have to become a professional like Cory. An amateur can have a wonderful time practicing.

CORY'S STORY

Cory loved women. He loved to talk to them, to look at them, but most of all he liked to touch them. From the moment he was old enough to know what a masseur was, he knew that was all he ever wanted to be.

Cory graduated from high school and then spent several years taking courses in massage. He traveled to Europe and Asia and studied with experts in the field. All the while, he practiced his art, earning money by giving massages. He developed strong, sinewy forearms and satiny soft skin on his hands.

In all that time, he never violated his massage ethics. His massages were always professional. His face was immobile while he stroked and kneaded the firm flesh of his female clients, never letting his hands move in an erotic manner.

Of course, Cory massaged men, too, but their skin was never as soft and their bodies were never as beautiful as those of his female clients.

And they always smelled so wonderful. He used scented massage oil, perfumed with essences of exotic flowers and spices that he had collected on his travels. He had blended special scents for many of his regular customers and sometimes, late at night, he would uncork a bottle of oil and it would bring back the feel of some particular woman's skin.

Cory's attitude toward erotic massage changed one afternoon, and it was Lilia that changed it.

Lilia had been introduced to Cory by another of his customers and she had been coming to him once a week for several months. She had skin the color of light coffee, smooth and without a blemish. Her legs were long, her stomach flat, and her flesh firm and supple to his touch. Her small breasts were tipped with large dark brown aureolas and constantly erect nipples.

A few days earlier, Cory had completed weeks of work on a special scent for Lilia. It smelled of cactus flowers and sagebrush and reminded him of dark nights in a silent desert. That afternoon, as he rubbed her back, he could almost feel the cool of the desert night. He closed his eyes and floated on the desert breeze as his hands pressed and kneaded, loosening all the muscles in Lilia's beautiful shoulders and neck.

She had been facedown for almost an hour before he sighed and whispered, "Turn over."

Lilia stretched and, with sensuous catlike movements, turned over. As usual, she was totally naked, but Cory didn't notice. His appreciation of women was centered in his hands. When she settled on her back, Cory poured a small pool of oil in his palm and slathered it over both of his hands.

He started by spreading oil on her feet and then he rubbed and pulled at each toe. He dug his fingers in at the base of her toes and into the arch of her foot. He felt rather than heard her purr.

He worked his way up her legs, rubbing her calves and thighs. He took ten minutes to make his way up to her belly. Then he touched her breasts. She lay completely relaxed with her arms at her sides as he slid his fingers over the flesh around her nipples.

"Why do you never touch my nipples?" Lilia said suddenly.

"It isn't professional," he said flatly.

"What if I asked you to? What if I asked you to touch me *all* over?"

His hands continued to caress her. He would love to touch her intimately, but it wasn't proper. Was it?

"Would you like me to touch you that way?" he asked, his voice barely above a whisper.

Lilia's eyes opened and she gazed at him. "I would like that very much," she whispered. "I would like to give my body up to you so you can make love to me with those wonderful hands of yours."

Cory hesitated. He absently fondled Lilia's breasts as if undecided. He wanted to do as she wished, but the ethics of his profession prevented him from doing so. A war raged within him while Lilia lay, eyes closed, totally relaxed. It was several minutes before he finally decided. His fingers danced over her breasts, then moved toward their darker-colored center. He pulled up on the erect tissue and was rewarded with a moan of pleasure.

His enjoyment of the feel of her flesh under his hands was suddenly totally different. He knew that he was giving her pleasure of a new kind. He was making love to her with his hands.

He worked his way back down to her belly, pressing spots that he had learned about from a master in Europe. He remembered the massage master's words.

"These pressure points I am going to show you are to be used only with a woman and then only if you have a desire to excite her sexually. They will give her tremendous pleasure, but they will create great hunger, as well. If you touch her in the way I will show you, you must be ready to complete the task, to show her the ultimate pleasure of orgasm with your hands."

He had watched and learned, mastering the techniques so he could pleasure his wife or lover. He had never thought to use them on his clients.

He used them now, however. He dug his thumb

deep into a special spot on Lilia's lower belly and heard her gasp. Then he reached deep down with the knuckle of his index finger, pressing on a particular location. He slid his hands around her waist and manipulated the bones in the small of her back.

Lilia's moans were almost continuous now and her thighs were parted, inviting his fingers to enter the forbidden zone between. If he had had any doubts about erotic massage, they vanished with the first brush of his fingertips over the curls between her legs.

He ran his fingers through her pubic hair and pushed on the bone beneath. He felt her hips press upward and her back arch. He was in heaven.

He kept rubbing with one hand while he reached for the oil with the other. He took the bottle and poured a slow trickle of oil onto Lilia's pubic mound and watched it flow into her wet vaginal folds. His fingers followed.

He carefully explored every crease and massaged her hot, swollen skin. She reached out, pulled his wrist, and tried to press his fingers into her wide opening.

"You're making me so hot," Lilia whispered.

"Be patient. Let me use my hands to give you pleasure like you've never had before. Surrender your body, your pleasure to me." He knew he wanted that as he had never wanted anything.

Her hand fell back to her side and she took a deep, shuddering breath.

Cory rubbed the oil into her clitoris, massaging

and squeezing her. Then he teased her opening with the tips of his fingers. He pulled at her inner lips with one hand while the other caressed the seldom-touched flesh just inside.

Her hips thrust upward, trying to catch his fingers and pull them inside.

"Yes, little one," he said hoarsely. "I know how much you want me. And you shall have me, right now."

On the word *now,* Cory thrust three fingers inside of her, filling her cunt. He pulled back and thrust again. He fucked her with his fingers while he massaged her clit with the other hand.

She screamed as she climaxed and writhed against his hands.

Still breathing heavily, Lilia smiled up at him. "Thank you, Cory. That was so beautiful. You have truly magic hands."

A large grin split Cory's face. "I'm so glad I could give you pleasure. Thank you for helping me understand that it's all right to make love to you."

Lilia smiled back at him and sat up. "Do we still have an appointment next week?"

He helped her down from the table and into her robe. "I wouldn't miss it for the world."

9
DIRTY TALK

"I love it when you talk dirty to me" has become a bad joke. It isn't. It can be terribly erotic to listen to your partner use sexual words: "I want to fuck your pussy," or "I love to suck your big cock." It can also be fun to "be forced" to say those words yourself.

Check the ads in any sexy magazine and you will see that there are people making a lot of money from dirty talk. Ad after ad suggests that you call "Mistress Whoever" and she'll tell you what you want to hear. Mike found out about the power of explicit talk from his office mate. Then he shared his understanding with his wife.

MIKE AND JOANNA'S STORY

Thirty-two-year-old Mike had been married to Joanna for eleven years. They had a good marriage, which had produced three children—two girls and a boy. Mike, an accountant, wore thick glasses over his myopic brown eyes and was just a bit over-weight. He prided himself on the fact that he still wore the same size slacks that he had worn ten years ago, but he did wear them slung a bit lower.

One dull afternoon, Alex, Mike's office mate, said softly, "You'll never guess what I did last week while you were away. I dialed one of these phone-sex numbers. Have you ever listened?"

Mike had never considered such a thing. It sounded vulgar and disgusting. His face must have sent a disapproving message to Alex.

"Don't knock it 'til you've tried it," Alex said as he crossed the room and closed the door. "Wait 'til you hear this." He dialed the phone and pressed the speaker button.

At first, Mike tried to ignore the words and sounds that came out of the speaker. No one should be turned on by language like that spoken by some nameless recording, he thought. Certainly *he* wasn't. Was he? As the moments passed, he found himself listening, entranced, while his cock grew hard in his slacks. When the call ended, all he could say was, "I didn't know that stuff was legal on the phone."

"You'd be amazed," Alex said. "I've tried several of these numbers. Last night, I had my wife listen. Wowie. We fucked like bunnies all night. You and Joanna should try it."

Mike quickly turned away. Alex shook his head and muttered, "Don't put it down too fast. You'd be amazed what it does for the sex life."

A little later, Mike excused himself and, in a stall in the men's room, replayed much of the tape in his mind. The dirty words and sounds made him crazy with hunger. He concentrated on the sound of the girl murmuring "I love it when you stick your big cock into me" while he stroked his hard penis to orgasm.

When he returned to his office, he got the phone number from Alex. For the next few days, anytime he had a few moments to spare, Mike called and listened. He bought a few X-rated magazines and, over the next few months, developed an extensive collection of phone numbers, each with its own specialty.

He found that he loved the sound of *cunt* and *cock* and *pussy*. He would say the words in his mind while he made love to his wife. Usually the phrase *I love to fuck your pussy* would drive him over the edge.

It never occurred to Mike, however, to share his enjoyment of dirty language with his wife. Not

Joanna. She never even said *shit,* or *piss off.* Joanna
still said *darn* when she stubbed her toe.

Joanna was short, slender, and had a head covered with unruly dark brown curls. She had been
brought up in an upper-class neighborhood in
Manhattan. Her parents, particularly her mother,
had been very proper, even prudish. Sometimes
Joanna wondered whether her parents had ever
had any fun in bed. Fortunately, she had always
liked sex with Mike, finding it both enjoyable and
satisfying.

One evening, Mike and Joanna were in bed
reading. Mike had spent half an hour on the phone
that afternoon, listening to a new recording on one
of his favorite phone-sex lines. Although he had
masturbated twice, he was still hungry for his wife.

Since they spoke very little during sex, Mike
liked some sound in the bedroom, so he reached
over and flipped on the radio. Soft easy-listening
music filled the room. He put his book on the bed
table and rolled over toward his wife. Gently, he
removed the magazine from Joanna's hands and
set it aside. Joanna giggled, knowing exactly what
Mike had in mind. Mike touched his mouth to
Joanna's lips as she snuggled down lower in the
bed.

Their arms wrapped around each other and they
kissed. As Joanna stroked Mike's back, his mouth
roamed her face. He kissed her closed eyes and
the tip of her nose. He nibbled on her earlobe and
kissed his way down the side of her neck, licking

the tender spot where her neck joined her shoulder.

As he swirled his tongue on her neck, he unbuttoned the front of her robe and slipped the straps of her nightgown down to reveal her shapely breasts. I love your titties, he said in his mind.

He kneaded the small mounds of white flesh and slid his tongue over their dark centers. He watched her nipples harden, and when the tight tips reached for his mouth, he drew first one and then the other into his mouth. He licked and bit down gently as Joanna's body moved against him in response.

"It makes my cock so hard when I suck your titties," he said.

It wasn't until he felt Joanna's body stiffen and pull away that Mike realized he had spoken aloud. He felt his cock soften and he rolled away so his back was toward his wife. He was totally embarrassed and completely tongue-tied.

Joanna was flabbergasted. She wanted to pretend that she hadn't heard, but that was impossible. Her body had reacted automatically. She wasn't sure what to say and she found that she wasn't sure how she felt. It wasn't ladylike to enjoy listening to *those* words, but she was wise enough to admit that they had excited her. But that was silly. Nice girls didn't listen to that kind of language. She couldn't imagine her mother ever allowing those words to be spoken in her presence. But what was really wrong with that kind of talk? She could feel the wetness between her legs. Her body enjoyed the words.

She knew that what had just happened had affected Mike deeply and she knew that what she said now might change their sex life for a long time. "Mike," she said softly, "I've never heard you use that kind of language before . . . but it's very exciting."

Mike almost missed what Joanna had said. It took moments for her words to penetrate.

He wasn't sure he'd understood. "What did you say?" he asked.

Joanna swallowed hard. "I said that I found what you said very exciting." She ran her fingertips over his back.

Mike rolled back toward Joanna. He held her hands and found that they were trembling. He looked into her eyes. "You aren't turned off?"

"I think I should be," she said, her voice barely audible, "but it's really the exact opposite."

Mike slid his hand across her shoulder and toward an erect nipple. He took a deep breath. It was going to be okay. "You like the word *titty*?"

Mike heard Joanna make a small sound deep in her throat and watched her eyes close. He pulled at her erect nipple. "And you like it when I suck your tits?"

Joanna wanted. She didn't know exactly what she wanted but she knew a kind of hunger that she seldom had felt before. She tangled her fingers in his hair and pulled his mouth tightly against her nipple.

Mike knew what he wanted. He wanted to hear her say those words. He wanted it so much that he was willing to take a big risk. He knew that she was very excited and he spent the next few moments doing everything he knew would increase her hunger. While he sucked and kneaded one breast, he slid his hand down her soft belly and slipped one finger into her wetness. She was moaning and lifting her hips in the same rhythm as his strokes of her clitoris. He lifted his head.

"Do you want me?" he whispered as he pressed one finger slightly into her.

She nodded and purred.

"How much?" Mike asked, the rhythm of his finger increasing.

"A lot. Please," Joanna whispered.

"Please what?" Mike saw Joanna's eyes open and he watched as she suddenly understood. "Please what, darling?"

"Please, I want you."

Mike smiled. He could feel her need and her excitement. His cock was swollen and he needed to plunge into her, but he knew that if he waited he might get exactly what he desired most. "That's not enough," he said softly. "I want to hear you say the words. I want you to say, 'Please fuck me.'"

"I can't say that," Joanna whispered, her voice hoarse and shaking.

"That's what you want, isn't it?"

Joanna nodded.

Mike's finger continued its rubbing of Joanna's clitoris and swollen, wet lips. "Then say it."

Joanna was going crazy. She tried to climax, holding herself and concentrating on her body, but satisfaction wouldn't come. She wanted Mike inside of her. "I want you to . . . "

Mike was tempted to let her have what she wanted but he was so close. "Fuck. Say the word."

"Oh baby," she whimpered, "I want you to . . . to fuck me."

Mike couldn't get his erect cock inside of her fast enough. With just a few strokes, he came, pulling Joanna with him.

They lay together until their bodies calmed. "You know how exciting that was," Mike whispered.

Joanna giggled. "I figured that out."

"For you, too?"

"I hate to admit how exciting that was. My mother would never understand."

They laughed as the picture of Joanna's very proper mother flashed through their minds. Mike laughed and said, "I won't tell if you don't." Then he became serious. "I want what happened this evening to happen again."

Joanna smiled. "I shouldn't say this, but I want that, too."

10

ANAL SEX

Anal sex is a game that can lead to misunderstandings. Many find the idea repugnant; others might like to fantasize but not participate. (I will discuss some problems with anal sex after this story. For now, just consider anal sex another game worth thinking about.)

Tom and Jenny discovered a mutual interest in anal sex when cable TV arrived in their area. They discovered that they not only wanted to watch, they wanted to play.

TOM AND JENNY'S STORY

Tom and Jenny were delighted when their housing development finally was wired for cable television.

The day the man from Windowvision arrived, they signed for all the available channels, including X-rated Channel 14.

Four weeks later, the truck arrived, cut the necessary tiny slit in the front lawn, and installed the wire. Both the TV in the living room and the one in their bedroom were quickly connected. The man who did the installation showed them how to work the cable boxes and the remote controls. Jenny signed the papers and sat in the living room for the rest of the afternoon, switching from channel to channel, enjoying the perfect picture and reveling in her newly acquired access to three movie channels.

It wasn't until the following Saturday night that Tom and Jenny got to enjoy cable TV from their bed. They watched a movie that both of them had wanted to see and then watched the eleven o'clock news. Since neither of them was tired, Tom started to switch the channels to see what else they might watch.

When Tom got to Channel 14, he caught a glimpse of an obviously X-rated movie. He hesitated and glanced over at Jenny. When she didn't protest, he left the movie on.

Jenny was embarrassed. She had seen a few "skin flicks" when she was in college, but that had been twenty years ago and those films had been no worse than *Animal House*. She was constantly amazed by what they were now allowed to show in the neighborhood movie theater. What was on the TV screen now was much worse. Or better.

Despite her embarrassment, she was fascinated. They were doing things on the screen that she had read about in trashy novels but had never actually witnessed.

The scene on TV was of a man and a woman next to a large swimming pool. The woman was stretched out in a long chair and the man was comfortably settled between her legs. Since the picture was taken from behind the man's head, Jenny couldn't see exactly what his mouth was doing, but she could guess that he was sensuously licking the woman's vagina and clitoris. His long slow strokes were obviously pleasing the woman. Her head was thrown back and her hands were buried in his hair, holding his head tightly against her.

Jenny looked over at Tom as she tried to gauge his reaction. He was leaning back against the pillows, watching the screen. His hands caressed the satin edging of the blanket in the same rhythm as the man's tongue caressed the woman on TV.

Jenny and Tom had been married for nineteen years. Early in their marriage, before the children, their sex life had been wonderful. They had made love in the front seat of cars, in the living room of his apartment when his parents were out, anyplace where they could find the time and the privacy.

In the last few years, sex had become perfunctory. Once a week, Tom would indicate that he was in the mood, Jenny would indicate that it was okay with her, and they would stroke and fondle each other for ten or fifteen minutes, then they would have intercourse.

As Jenny watched the screen, the man picked his head up and began to lick his index finger. "You want it," he said as the woman stared at his hand, "don't you?"

"Yes," she cried out. "Stick it in me."

Jenny thought that he was going to push his finger inside of her vagina, but she was wrong. The man grabbed the woman's ankles and draped her legs over his shoulders. She couldn't see exactly, but she shivered as she realized that, as he licked her clit, he was pushing his finger into her ass.

Jenny had never thought seriously about how anal sex must feel, although it was now not the forbidden topic it once had been. It was obvious that many people, like the girl on the screen, found great pleasure in the practice.

The woman moved her hips and screamed with pleasure, and the excitement was contagious. Jenny was getting aroused as her mind replayed that initial insertion over and over.

Suddenly, she felt Tom close to her. "Did you enjoy that scene?" he asked, breathing softly in her ear.

She looked at Tom and blushed. It was like being caught reading a dirty magazine. She should deny it all. "No," she should say, "it looks disgusting." But that would be a lie.

"It's hard to talk about, isn't it?" Tom said.

Jenny nodded and swallowed.

"Then don't say anything." Tom was wildly excited as well. It had never occurred to him that something like that would excite his wife, but now, thinking about it, he couldn't keep his hands off her.

"Let's just agree to one thing," Tom said. "If I do anything that you don't like, just say 'Stop' and I will. Okay?"

Jenny nodded again. She was still afraid that if she opened her mouth, some denial of what she felt would come out.

With the sounds from the TV in the background, Tom leaned over and kissed his wife. Slowly, he explored her mouth with his tongue, taking time to enjoy the feel of her. As they kissed, he slowly ran his hands over her body. He reached up under her nightgown and brushed the palm of his hand over her breasts. Her nipples were already hard and fully erect. He had never felt her so excited so quickly.

He pulled her nightgown over her head and flipped the covers back. Then he pulled off his shorts and stretched out next to her and pressed the length of his body against her side.

He kept his hands sliding over her satiny skin, afraid that if he gave her time to think, she would change her mind. He stroked her chest and belly as his mouth found a nipple and sucked and nipped. Her hips moved under his hand and her thighs opened and invited him.

He slid his fingers between her legs, gliding over her incredibly wet cunt. He felt heat radiate from her like a furnace. He wanted to climb on top of her and ram his big erect cock into her, but he also wanted to wait. Just a little patience and he would try some things that he always had wanted to do.

He moved his body down the bed until his face was near her pubic hair. For a moment, he just looked at her beautiful cunt. He inhaled her fragrance and felt his penis getting harder.

Jenny felt his breath caress her between her legs. It's been so long since he did that to me, she thought, and it feels so good. She could still hear the movie in the background. She glanced at the screen. You're not the only one enjoying yourself, she said silently to the girl in the movie.

Tom leaned over and flicked his tongue over her clitoris. She made small sounds, deep in her throat, and pressed her hips upward, closer to his face. His tongue had a life of its own. He licked and stroked her with it, tasting her juices. Her clitoris was hard and swollen and every time he stroked it with his tongue, she shivered and he felt her muscles spasm.

He raised his head and looked at Jenny. Her head was thrashing back and forth and her eyes were tightly shut. He knew what he wanted to do but he was afraid of spoiling whatever it was that was happening. This was the most highly charged sex they had had in years. His mind, however, kept returning to that man on the TV who had his finger in the girl's ass.

He ran his fingers across Jenny's soaking wet cunt. Smoothly, he ran the tip of his finger backward, gently moving across her tight asshole. Her body jolted as he touched her there. His finger lingered, wetting her ass with her juices.

Jenny considered telling Tom to stop, but she

couldn't. She wanted to feel him filling her all over. She wanted it and she wasn't going to deny Tom or herself.

Anal intercourse had always been a large part of Tom's sexual fantasies. Sometimes he would wake up in the middle of the night from a dream in which his cock was buried in the ass of some faceless woman. Sweating and totally aroused, he would stumble into the bathroom, take out his swollen penis, and stroke himself to orgasm.

Now he stroked his wet finger across her tiny asshole and he pressed just a bit. Jenny can still tell me to stop, he thought. He watched for negative reactions, but Jenny's body was still thrashing around and he could hear her pant.

He pressed harder and his finger slipped a tiny bit into her ass. Gradually, his finger worked its way deeper and deeper. She felt like velvet as he fucked her ass with his finger. He didn't know whether his cock could stand much more, so he pulled his finger out and moved on top of Jenny.

"Yes, Tommy," she moaned, "love me." She hadn't called him Tommy since they were first married.

He rammed his cock deep inside of her and climaxed almost immediately. It was too quick, he thought. She's still so high.

He pulled out and began to stroke her again.

Jenny murmured, "You don't have to do that. I'm content." Her hips told a different story.

"Let me stroke you," he said.

"Mmmm," she purred. "Nice."

He returned to rhythmically stroking her clitoris

with one hand while a finger of his other hand again slowly explored her ass. Jenny was almost incoherent as Tom drove two fingers deep into her cunt, ramming her hard, fucking her with his fingers. The contrast between the fingers hard-fucking her cunt and his soft exploration of her ass was more than she could take.

Suddenly, her muscles tightened and waves of contraction engulfed Tom's fingers, deep within both her cunt and her ass.

"Yes," she screamed. "Oh, yes."

Her hips pounded hard against his hands. For long minutes, she was fucked with both Tom's hands and she was filled as never before. She screamed her pleasure over and over as waves of heat surged through her body.

When she calmed, he pressed the entire length of his body against hers.

"It's never been like that," Jenny said.

"I know," Tom said. "It was wonderful. I was so excited that I couldn't wait."

Jenny smiled. "That's quite a compliment."

Tom's eyes wandered back to the flickering screen, but Jenny reached across him and pressed the button on the remote control. The screen went blank. "There are so many more nights," she said.

○ ● ○

There are a few things that need clarification regarding anal sex. First, as you have seen, it is not

just a male homosexual experience. I was reluctant
to try anal sex the first time. I was sure it would hurt
me rather than give me pleasure. I tried it with a
partner who wanted it very much and I agreed,
primarily to give him pleasure. He had agreed
beforehand to stop at any point that I asked him to.
To my surprise, I found it extremely erotic, particularly when he combined it with vaginal or clitoral
stimulation. Another partner found that an anal
dildo stimulated parts of his anatomy that were not
usually stimulated.

A few words of caution. The vaginal passage is
relatively short and is closed at the interior end, so
dildos or other objects can penetrate only so far.
That is not true with anal penetration. Things can
penetrate so deeply that they may be difficult to
extricate, a very embarrassing situation that occasionally may necessitate hospital emergency room
assistance. If you're going to play, take care to use
a dildo with a wide flange at the end. And use only
dildos, not dildo substitutes. I needn't go into the
details of what can happen if you play this way with
the wrong items.

If you want to try anal intercourse, remember
that the anal passage is not lubricated the way the
vaginal one is. Severe injury can be caused by dry
penetration. Use K-Y jelly or a lubricated condom.

Whether lubricated or not, *always use a condom.*
Remember that the AIDS virus puts both you and
your partner at risk from every sexual partner that
either of you has had in the past five to ten years.
In addition, you can get a serious urinary infection

from just a small exposure to anal bacteria. Use a condom and avoid any risk.

And don't use the same condom to penetrate the vagina that has just been used in the anal passage. A woman can develop a nasty genital or urinary infection from her own anal bacteria. If you have had anal intercourse, take the old condom off and use a new one.

11

AVOIDING SOME PITFALLS

There is an old joke that illustrates the pitfalls of creative sex better than I could.

There was once a couple who had an adequate sex life, but occasionally, during lovemaking, the husband would ask his wife, "Just once, could we do it doggie style?"

"Never!" his wife would always say.

So throughout their long relationship, the husband was mildly frustrated. Finally, on his deathbed, the husband asked the wife, "Why did you always refuse to do it doggie style? What did you have against making love doggie style, on hands and knees?"

"Hands and knees!" his wife shouted, horrified. "I thought you meant out in the yard."

I guess the moral of that little story is, Never assume. If you are just beginning to venture into new areas of sexual activity, be sure you understand what your partner is trying to tell you. Be alert for signs that you might have misunderstood. Learn to read body language, and, when in doubt, despite your embarrassment, talk. In straightforward language.

Remember that the best words your partner could possibly hear are, "Yes, I really do want to do it that way," or, "Are you really interested in that, too? I was hoping you'd be."

During the past few years, I have experimented with many areas of off-center sex and I have learned a number of lessons, some the hard way. Based on my experiences, here are some warnings and tips I'd like to share with you so that you might avoid some of the pitfalls and awkward situations I've encountered. The topics that follow are in no particular order, so I recommend that you read the entire section. You never know which of these helpful hints you might use.

Laughter. There is one thing that is almost as important for successfully venturing into new types of sexual experiences as an open mind, and that is a sense of humor. You will make mistakes and get into predicaments that you never imagined, some erotic, some just funny. If it's funny, laugh. Enjoy sharing the joke with your partner. Don't take sex so seriously that you take all the fun out of it.

Sexual Prowess. I am a reader of romance novels. In them, in movies, and in erotic articles in magazines, men are always capable of multiple erections and women are capable of multiple orgasms, each as "exquisitely complete" as the last. They make love for hours, changing positions frequently, while she never gets frustrated and he never loses his erection. They make love three or four times in one night and only rarely come up for air. Naturally, I expected real people to perform like those I read about, and I was terribly disillusioned both by my partners and by myself. What was wrong with us? One good orgasm and all my partner and I wanted was to luxuriate in all of the soft, sharing feelings that follow wonderful lovemaking.

There are probably many people out there who are multiply orgasmic. I now have accepted that I'm not, and none of the men with whom I have had relationships are, either. Maybe they were at sixteen, but I haven't met a man capable of more than one or possibly two orgasms within a lovemaking session. There are probably men who can maintain an erection for hours, but I've never met one. And I know that none of this matters for a good lovemaking experience.

Be realistic. Don't expect miracles from your partner. More important, don't have unrealistic expectations about yourself. Enjoy the experiences you both have and don't measure them against what you believe they should be. On the other hand, don't deny the possibility of pleasures after that first orgasm. Stroking and kissing need not stop with a climax.

Sometimes orgasms don't happen at all. Sometimes that's all right. I often get so much pleasure out of a prolonged lovemaking session that, when my partner climaxes, it's like an orgasm for me, as well—not a physical orgasm but, rather, a mental one, and that's so satisfying that nothing more is necessary.

But sometimes that's not enough. Be aware of your partner and don't assume that because you've climaxed, she has. Try to be alert, even if she maintains that it's never been better. Women are often reluctant to make demands on a man who has just climaxed. She may think, He's tired now, or, He won't be interested. That's hogwash. Communicate.

Men, turn up your radar. Women, don't make him guess, but don't insult him, either. Ask gently for what you want, or take his hand and use it to show him what you need, or masturbate while he watches. Use one of the communication techniques I've explained in this book if you need to. And don't give up if your partner is slow to realize what you're trying to say.

There is an even greater mental problem about orgasms. I once knew a couple who had done a great deal of eating out over the years and considered themselves gourmets. Unfortunately, they spent most of each meal comparing that night's dishes with ones they had had in the past. Nothing was ever as good as the food they had had a few years ago at some other bistro. At that bistro years ago, they probably spoiled the meal comparing the food with some meal still further back.

You can spoil a sexual encounter by trying to

remember when it was better. Now is now and the past is past. Revel in the present and treasure your wonderful memories. If you have ideas for improving the future, use them to build on, not to undermine.

Shaving. Many women shave what has come to be called the bikini area, that tender area of pubic hair on the inside of the upper thigh and on the lower abdomen. Many also trim the length of their pubic hair. There is a star of X-rated movies who shaves her pubic hair in the shape of a heart. Some men and women find it erotic to make love to someone with a naked pubic area. Tastes vary.

If you have never shaved your pubic area, do so carefully. Nicks can be very painful and skin in the pubic area is very easily irritated. After you shave, wash the area with a disinfectant soap such as Betadine Surgical Scrub, or swab the area with alcohol or witch hazel, being careful of the mucous membranes.

I have never had my pubic area shaved except when I had my two children, which was quite a long time ago. I do remember, though, that it was very itchy as the hair grew. With these caveats, if shaving turns you and your partner on, go for it.

Carpets. If you've never made love on a rug before, be careful. Your elbows and your coccyx, or tailbone, are very vulnerable to rug burns. In the heat of passion, you might not even realize what's happening until you have large and very nasty abrasions. You might try lying on a large towel, which also prevents strange stains from appearing on your beautiful beige wall-to-wall. Worrying about such mundane things is a sure mood killer.

Drugs. Some thoughts about drugs. Sex is its own high. It can bring on levels of pleasure that can be reached in no other way. Hard drugs are totally unnecessary. As a matter of fact, they can be counterproductive. One friend who tried pot in the freewheeling sixties told me that when he tried to make love while high, he couldn't concentrate sufficiently on what he was doing to climax. Other hard drugs, such as cocaine, can make your nipples, penis, or vagina numb, limiting your appreciation of stimulation.

There are no aphrodisiacs that I'm aware of that are effective and not dangerous. Oysters, asparagus, and rhinoceros horn have no proven ability to do anything to enhance your potency. Spanish flies and their ilk are irritants and can be dangerous or even fatal.

In contrast, there are nonprescription drugs advertised in sex magazines. Read the ads carefully. Most contain only one active ingredient, caffeine. It's easier and less expensive to drink coffee, tea, or cola.

Other companies advertise placebo sex aids. The word *placebo* comes from the medieval Latin for pleasing or acceptable. It means something that has no pharmacological effect, no medical results: sugar pills. Remember that the most active and successful erogenous zone is your brain. If you want to pretend to give your partner something that will make him your sexual slave or make her so hungry for you that she'll jump you as soon as you get home, make sure your partner knows about it. Feed him sugar pills and plant the idea that you are going to indulge in some good active sex and he will be unable to resist you. Pretending can be great fun, but it needs cooperation.

If you feel you need something to increase your potency, take a "pill" and pretend that it has worked better than your wildest dreams. Get into it. If you cooperate with the sugar pill, it will work.

Spontaneity. Those who do not have to worry about birth control, for whatever reason, are able to make love whenever the fancy strikes them. Those of us who have to concern ourselves about not getting pregnant don't have that luxury. There are, however, things a woman can do to help.

If you are a diaphragm user, insert it every night after dinner (or whenever your usual loving time is). The same goes for contraceptive sponges. Don't think about it. Don't feel that it is a decision you have to make. Don't say "Well tonight I don't think he's in the mood, so I'll skip it." Moods change.

What do you have to lose? Of course, you can always stop for a moment to insert a birth-control device. A moment's pause sometimes refreshes and recharges. Sometimes having to stop is a mood killer. I hope your excitement isn't that delicate.

Condoms. There may be times when it is advisable for a man to wear a condom. In addition to preventing conception, condoms are excellent for protecting your partner from the spread of urinary-tract infections or sexually transmitted diseases. They can also make one or the other more comfortable during a time of genital irritation. As discussed, condoms must be used anytime you try anal sex.

Don't close your mind to condoms. Don't think of them as a deterrent to pleasure. I rather enjoy having my partner wear one, and we use them frequently. The moments that my partner spends putting on a condom are wonderful torture and can actually heighten my pleasure by making me wait for what is to come. While he is putting a condom on, he sometimes tells me what he is going to do to me when he is ready—step by step in wonderful detail.

Condoms have become increasingly easy to buy and use in the last few years. Every drugstore has many brands out on the shelves, singly and in packs of three, five, or a dozen.

Since the competition is heavy in this multi-million-dollar business, many improvements have been made. Condoms are no longer the heavy rubber sleeves that men summarily rejected as feeling like "washing your feet with your socks on." They are thinner than the condoms of the past and permit more delicate sensations. They come in many shapes, with ticklers and reservoirs on the end, in many textures, with ribs or raised rubber studs, and in colors that range from golden yellow to black. They come lubricated or dry, rolled or unrolled; one type even comes packed in a fortune cookie. Some magazines sell sampler packs of fifty or a hundred. If you are using them for protection, the only necessity is that the ones you use be leakproof. If they're just for fun, try the edible Kandie Kondoms I saw advertised recently.

My partner has always used the kind that are prelubricated, and the lubricant feels cold. I particularly enjoy the initial penetration when my muscles clench almost instinctively from the chill, giving us both an extra stimulation. In addition, there are times when the extra lubrication is welcome. Occasionally, I am not "dripping with love juice" for one reason or another, but I still want the feeling of my partner's penis inside of me. If this happens, I suggest that we use a condom. Then I don't feel threatened by my partner's erection and my lack of physical arousal.

Children. Don't play sexual games with the children around unless you're sure they won't interrupt. Nothing reduces the passion level more quickly than the sound of someone at the bedroom door asking for a glass of water. If some little person should knock, however, tell him that you are having some personal time and that you'll emerge in an hour. Put a hook on your bedroom door, high up and out of reach of little hands.

Reading Material. The last few chapters of this book discuss erotica for both foreplay and communication. They also contain many erotic stories, written both to excite and instruct. You might want to explore the erotic reading matter in bookstores and on magazine racks. Much is available by mail. Beware. Many of these books and magazines use language that is a lot more explicit than the language I use and many of them describe situations that are much more offbeat than those I will illustrate. Be selective with what you share, particularly if you and your partner are still new to erotic literature. Some of those words and situations might be a complete turnoff. Warn your partner and explain that it is particularly important not to misunderstand or overreact. And if something does offend either of you, discard it and try something else.

12

BEDTIME STORIES

I hope you have added bookmarking to your other communication tools. Here are some stories that can be used in a different way. They are read-alouds or act-outs, stories to heighten your sensuality. They're fantasies, adventures in erotica.

By now, you may realize there are things that would be fun to try and there are things that are exciting only to fantasize or read about. The difference is most important.

A common female fantasy is rape, although no woman wants to actually be raped. The rape they imagine is forceful but nonviolent and nonpainful, usually done by someone they find physically attractive. Actual rape is abhorrent to any woman.

Many people enjoy fantasies in which they are watched by others while they make love, or in which they participate in sex with multiple partners. Although these are not monogamous activities, the fantasies can enhance your lovemaking.

The first way to use these nonmonogamous fantasies is to read or tell a story to your partner. Maybe you'd both enjoy a situation in which a woman is loved by several men at a time or during which several couples undress and an orgy ensues. Lie in bed with a glass of wine and some soft music. Open to a story at random or select one you already know. Read it aloud to your partner or read alternate paragraphs.

I hear you saying, "It's embarrassing to say those things out loud." You're right, but it's a titillating embarrassment. It's erotic and incredibly exciting. It's verbal foreplay. I will bet that if you start a story that excites both of you, you won't finish it.

The second way to enjoy this type of activity is to act out a story. Pretend that your partner has become a different person partway through a lovemaking session and that he now has a different personality or is a different age or physical type. Pretend that the wizard is watching you through the curtains. Pretend that the sultan's harem and guards are participating in your lovemaking. Pretend. . .

THE MAGIC CRYSTAL

Once upon a time in a faraway land lived a magician with extraordinary powers. It was said that he could make water run uphill, turn night into day, and turn lead into gold. People paid him handsomely for his magic potions and ointments, which, it was said, could cure everything from blindness to a bad cold.

The wizard was not an old man, but he had lived a long time and he had seen much. He had had three wives, each a worse nag than the last. Now, he satisfied himself with an occasional wench, and he had a housekeeper named Gabriella to take care of his suite of rooms in the king's castle.

One day, Gabby was cleaning his workroom while he developed a particularly potent ointment to cure the king's swollen, aching foot.

"Sir," Gabby said, "could I ask you something?"

The magician looked up. Gabby had been working for him for over six months and this was the first time she had asked anything of him.

"What can I do for you, child?"

"What would it cost for you to make me a potion? Something that would make me attractive to men."

"But you are a very lovely girl. What do you need with a potion?"

"Look at me. No man will take a second look at me."

The wizard looked at the girl carefully. Despite the desperate look on her face, she was not at all unattractive. She had deep gray eyes and smooth skin the color of ripe apricots. She also had a beautiful smile, which, the magician realized, he had seen very seldom. His eyes roamed lower and took in her drab dress and her slouched posture. He had no real idea what her body looked like under her shapeless clothes.

"My dear," he said at long last, "what, exactly, is your trouble?"

"I want to be beautiful. I want men to fall at my feet." She blushed. "I want them to . . . you know, want me."

The magician smiled. "I think I know what you want. But I'm afraid that it would cost a great deal."

Gabby slumped even deeper in her seat. "I have very little money."

The magician had a good idea of how easy it would be to turn this duckling into a seductive woman, and he knew exactly what he wanted in return. "There are other ways to pay besides money," he said.

Gabby looked puzzled, but interested, as the wizard continued. "I could make you a magic crystal that would make you irresistible to men," he said softly, "but you would have to agree to my conditions. You would not owe me any money."

Gabby's face lit up. "What would I have to do?" she asked, knowing the answer. She was willing to do anything, to let the wizard use her body in return for the crystal he promised to make for her.

"You would have to bring a man up here to this room. I will secrete myself in the small room behind that curtain and watch you make love."

Gabby looked puzzled. "You don't want to have me?" she asked.

"No, my dear. I just want to watch you and some handsome man make love right here in my work-room."

"Is that really all?" Gabby asked. She looked into the wizard's eyes. "I think I would enjoy having you watch me, if that's what you want. I wouldn't have to tell anyone, would I? It would be our secret."

"It would be our secret. You would be perform-ing, just for me. Come back in three days and I'll have something ready for you. I'll also have some suitable clothes and a few other things."

For Gabby and the wizard, the three days passed as if the minutes were being carried by turtles. Finally, on the afternoon of the third day, Gabby washed her hair until it gleamed like burnished copper and scrubbed her body until it tingled. Then she went to the magician's studio, where she found the wizard seated at his workbench.

"Go behind that screen, my dear," he said, "and put on the clothes you will find there. Then I will give you the magic."

Gabby scampered behind the screen. She

gasped when she saw the beautiful clothes laid out. There was a blouse of a lacy black fabric that felt like gossamer as she put it on. It fell low, just covering the tops of her dark brown nipples. There was a red skirt, full and ruffled, with three fluffy petticoats. There were tiny black slippers and long golden earrings that hung down to her shoulders and brushed her skin as she moved.

"There's a brush for your hair and some makeup for your lips and cheeks," the wizard said, "and a flagon of scent that will enhance the magic. There's also a small mirror for you to use."

"It's too small for me to see what I look like," Gabby said.

"Just make your face up as best you can. Then, after I've given you my magic, you can look at yourself."

Quickly, Gabby made up her face. When she stepped from behind the screen, the wizard knew that his magic would work. The girl wasn't beautiful, but she had a sultry sensuality that would drive men wild. All she had to do was use it.

With great ceremony, the magician took a black velvet pouch from inside his robe. Slowly, he opened the drawstring and withdrew a golden chain on which hung a pink crystal, about the size of his thumb. Around the crystal, gold wire was wound in an intricate design. "Turn around so I can put this around your neck," the magician said.

He placed the chain around Gabby's neck. As he knew it would, the crystal nestled in the hollow between her ample breasts.

"This is a magic crystal," he said solemnly. "While you wear it, you will be irresistible to men. But you must take care and use it sparingly. And remember our bargain."

"Oh yes, sir," Gabby said. "Can I look at myself now?"

"There is a glass over there," the magician said. He watched as Gabby walked toward the mirror. She walked upright, with her large breasts thrust forward. There was a seductive swing to her hips.

When she looked at herself in the glass, she smiled. She turned left and right as she examined every aspect of her enticing body. She liked what she saw. "Yes," she murmured, "I will be irresistible."

"Is there someone special you want to be irresistible for?" the wizard asked.

"I have always liked Will, one of the King's gardeners," she said with a slight blush, "but he has never noticed me. If he held me, I would be in heaven."

"Shall I get him up here for you?" the magician asked. "Then we can complete our bargain."

"Oh, yes," Gabby said. "I would like that."

The wizard summoned the gardener, hid himself in the side room, and waited. He didn't have to wait long.

Will walked into the studio. He was a tall, slender young man with large brown eyes and slightly bucked teeth. He looked around but saw no one. "You wanted to see me, wizard?" he said loudly.

"I wanted to see you," Gabby said as she walked from behind the screen.

"Who . . . who are you?" Will stammered, unable to look away from the girl's fantastic body. His eyes watched her hips sway seductively as she walked. Then he looked a little higher and gazed at her unconfined breasts under her lacy blouse.

"I'm Gabriella," she said. "Don't you recognize me?"

"Gabriella. Is it really you? Y-y-you look so different."

"It's the crystal." She pulled the chain and dangled the crystal in front of her breasts. "It's beautiful, isn't it?"

Will could only nod.

"Come closer so you can have a better look." The magic was obviously working well. Gabby could see the unmistakable look of lust in Will's eyes.

When he didn't seem able to move, she walked closer. "See," she said softly, "the crystal almost glows."

In the side room, the wizard smiled. He also was having a difficult time tearing his eyes away from the crystal and Gabby's beautiful body, her long legs and wide hips.

Gabby came so close to Will that the tips of her breasts brushed the front of his shirt. "See how the gold is woven around the outside," she said. Her lips were so close to Will's that he could feel her hot breath and smell her fragrance.

With her breasts touching his chest and her

mouth so close to his, he could resist no longer. Hungrily, he reached his hand around the back of Gabby's neck and pressed his lips against hers. His tongue reached deep into her mouth to drink in her sweetness. His other hand pressed the small of her back, forcing the length of her body against him.

She felt his erection pressing against her belly. Yes, she thought, the crystal is making me irresistible. Over Will's muscular shoulder, Gabby looked at the curtain and knew the wizard was behind it. In return for his magic, I must reward the wizard with a good show, she thought.

She pulled away and smiled at Will. "Do you find me beautiful?" she asked.

"You are so beautiful," Will said, wishing he knew the fancy words to say.

Gabby slowly pulled down the front of her blouse so her large breasts spilled out. "What about my breasts. Are they beautiful, too?" As Will reached for her, Gabby danced out of his reach and played with her breasts, always facing the room, from where she knew the wizard was watching. She alternately extended her breasts toward Will and backed away.

When her back touched the magician's worktable, she stopped and let Will catch her. He bent down and took her already-swollen nipple in his mouth. He kneaded her flesh with both of his hands as he suckled hungrily.

As he sucked, Gabby saw the curtain in front of the wizard's hiding place stir. She knew that he could see well through the space between the panels, but she wanted to see the effect the scene was having on him. She motioned to him to open the curtains.

Will's back was to the magician and the young man was fully occupied playing with Gabby's breasts. In response to Gabby's gesture, the wizard pulled the curtain aside. Then he opened the front of his robe and showed Gabby his erection. Gabby quickly realized that it was even larger than the one she had felt in the front of Will's pants. The magician's gaze locked with Gabby's as he wrapped his hand around his penis and stroked himself.

Gabby looked down at Will's head as he sucked, then up at the wizard's hand pumping his engorged cock. It's like making love to two men at the same time, she thought.

Silently, the wizard stepped back and let the curtain fall, but Gabby could see it flutter slightly as the wizard stroked himself. Will switched to the other breast and sucked and squeezed, but it wasn't enough. Gabby wanted more.

She pulled herself up onto the table and sat on the edge. Slowly, she raised her skirt to reveal first her calves, then her knees and thighs.

When the skirt rested at her waist, she leaned back on her elbows on the table. She moved her hips in a circle and watched Will's eyes, which never left her tiny lace underpants. She teased him with her hips and beckoned to him.

Will looked into her eyes for a moment, then gently placed his fingers against the crotch of her panties. It was soaked and the wetness made him even more anxious to possess Gabby. Suddenly, he grabbed her and pulled the panties off. With one hand playing with each nipple, he bent his head to the curly hair between her legs.

Gabby hadn't had much experience with men and loving, so she was completely surprised by the violence of her body's reaction to Will's tongue on her. It was as though there was a flame consuming her vagina, burning but not hurting. As the tip of Will's tongue slid along the folds of her skin, she shuddered.

As the wizard watched, he stroked his rigid cock and slid his tongue over his lips.

Will tasted her wetness and began to flick his tongue over her swollen clit. The sensations drove her wild. She started to close her eyes and surren-der to the pleasure, but she stopped herself. She looked over Will's head toward the curtain.

Once more, it lifted and she saw the magician, his penis extending from the front of his open robe while his hand pumped. She watched him stroke and fondle himself while Will gently sucked her pulsating clit into his mouth. His rhythmic sucking and the wizard's stroking combined to create an irresistible force.

"Be inside of me," she cried, both to Will and to the magician. "I need you to love me now!"

Will remained unaware of the magician. The handsome young man tore off his breeches and, still standing beside the table, drove his engorged penis deep into Gabby's steaming cunt. Over and over he thrust, until she could feel him start to come. She looked over his shoulder at the wizard and licked her lips. She mimed the motion of her mouth sucking his cock.

Gabby saw the wizard come, the thick cream spewing from him. Her muscles reacted to the sight of the wizard's orgasm and her movements caused Will to climax also. As both Will and the wizard came, so did Gabby.

Will collapsed on top of her as the curtain fell in front of the wizard's room.

A while later, Will promised to meet Gabby in the same room the following afternoon, then left.

As the door closed behind Will, the wizard took a step from behind the curtain. His robes were back in order and his face was calm. "You know that you made all this happen. You and only you. You understand that the crystal has no power, don't you?" he said.

"Yes," she said. "I think I understand."

"Good," the magician said. "It was the way you behaved that attracted Will, not any power of the crystal."

"Will wasn't the only man to enjoy this afternoon," she said with a smile. "I think I excited you both, but I'll wear the crystal tomorrow, anyway. I have some things in mind that I think both you and Will can enjoy."

The magician smiled back at her and touched the curtain. "You know where I'll be."

○ · ● ○

THE QUEEN'S FOOTMEN

Once upon a time, there was a queen of a small country. Twenty-four-year-old Queen Gloria was lonely. Her husband, King Francis, was a good king, but he was over sixty years old and he had not been very healthy the last few years. He had married Gloria eight years earlier when the previous queen died. Queen Theresa had given the king seven daughters, but he needed a son to succeed him. Gloria had given the king four sons in the first five years, and now that she had served her function, the king paid little attention to her.

Gloria had been a virgin when she married King Francis, but she quickly learned to love a good fuck. Unhappily, it had been quite a while since her last climax. The four little princes were taken care of by a retinue of nurses and nannies, so the queen was not only frustrated, she was bored. Therefore, to relieve her ennui, she decided to pay a visit to her parents, the baron and baroness of a nearby kingdom.

One beautiful spring morning, Queen Gloria set out in her coach with a driver and two footmen. It would be a full day's ride, so they were well supplied with baskets of food and small casks of good local wine.

They drove along quietly for several hours, but even though the coach was well sprung, Gloria was soon sore and annoyed with her confinement. She decided that she would put up with the bumpy ride only so long, so even before the sun was directly overhead, Queen Gloria motioned to one of her footmen who rode alongside the coach.

"Paul," Gloria said, "I know a lovely spot to stop for lunch. Tell Mark to look for a small roadway on the right, just after that stand of trees ahead. At the end of the road, there's a lovely meadow with a stream running through it."

"Yes, my lady," the footman said. As he galloped forward, Gloria gazed at his strong thighs hugging his horse's sides. He's a very attractive young man, she thought. Very attractive indeed. She put her pinky in her mouth and sucked it as she wondered, I couldn't, could I?

A few moments later, the coach pulled off the main road and bumped down a rutted dirt path. The pounding of the coach cushions against her sore bottom convinced her. What good is being queen if I can't have a bit of fun? she thought.

The coach pulled to a stop and the footmen dismounted. Paul and Mark, the driver, got the heavy hamper from under the driver's seat while Tom, the other footman, opened the carriage door and helped Gloria down from the coach.

For the first time, Queen Gloria took a careful look at her retinue. Tom was not overly tall and he had a small, slender frame, blond hair, light eyes, and a quick smile that caused twin dimples to appear in his cheeks.

Paul was dark and tall. He had broad shoulders, wide hips, and a slender waist, which complimented them. His mustache was as dark as his shoulder-length hair, which was cut with bangs across his severe forehead. His eyes were dark, his nose straight. He's really rather handsome, Gloria thought.

Then there was Mark, the driver. His hair was brown and shaggy, like the coats of his horses. As the three men spread a large cloth for her to sit on, Queen Gloria noticed that Mark's hands were tremendous, calloused, and rough. His hands are so big, but they look so gentle in spite of their size, she thought. It's amazing that I've taken these men for granted for so long.

The three men set out the queen's meal and then laid out some food for themselves a few feet away.

"I am going to be very lonely if I sit here by myself," she said as she settled herself gracefully on the cloth. "Why don't you sit with me?" she asked.

"We couldn't do that," Paul said. "It wouldn't be proper."

"It might not be proper," the queen said, "but it's my command. And it would be less proper to disobey your queen."

"No ma'am. It would not be possible for us to disobey a royal command," the three said as they brought their meal over.

The men, dressed in their sparkling purple and gold uniforms, settled themselves on the cloth. Slowly, they got over their uneasiness and soon the four were enjoying a good time, laughing and talking. When they had finished the first small cask of wine, Gloria had the men open a second one. As the wine was consumed, the conversation got more spirited.

"Your Majesty has a good sense of humor," Tom said.

"I wish you would stop calling me Your Majesty," Gloria said. "My name is Gloria. I would like you to use it, if only for this afternoon."

"Yes, Your Majesty," Tom said. Gloria frowned. Paul cleared his throat. "I mean yes, Gloria," he said.

A wide smile lit Gloria's face. "That's better." The three men appreciated what her smile did for her good looks.

As they finished the second cask of wine in the warm sun, the men started to look exceedingly uncomfortable in their hot uniforms. "Why don't you remove your jackets," Queen Gloria suggested.

"It would not be proper, Your Highness," Paul said.

"It most certainly would," Gloria said, "because I say so."

"But Gloria," Paul continued, "we don't have shirts on. These jackets are too tight to allow us to wear anything underneath."

"I've seen men before," Queen Gloria said. "I

don't want to arrive at my parents' castle with sweaty attendants. If I say it's all right, it is, and that's all there is to that."

Without any delay, the three men removed their jackets. Queen Gloria spent long minutes just appreciating their beauty. Paul was hairless, but his upper body was well muscled; straight blond hair covered Tom's well-developed chest; while Mark had heavy curly black hair on his chest, and huge shoulders.

"I guess you have those muscles from driving my horses all day," Gloria said, unable to tear her eyes away from Mark's body.

"I guess so," Mark said.

"You don't talk much, either, do you, Mark?"

"I guess I prefer talking to horses."

Queen Gloria smiled. "Are horses as beautiful as I am?" Gloria reached up and pulled out the scarf that had held her long blond hair. It spilled in waves across her shoulders and down the front of her gown.

"No ma'am," Mark said. "No one is as beautiful as you are."

Paul and Tom also were looking at her, not as their beautiful queen, but as a beautiful woman. Her face was small and perfectly oval and her eyes were green like summer grass. Her lips were full and each man yearned to be the one to kiss them.

"The king isn't around much anymore," Gloria said, "and I'm very lonely."

"Oh no, ma'am," the men said. "You shouldn't ever be lonely."

Gloria pulled off her satin slippers and her white silk stockings. "I guess loneliness is just one of those burdens a queen must bear," she said with a sigh.

After a moment, she said, "I have an idea. Why don't you remove your boots and wade in the stream with me. The cool water would feel so good, wouldn't it?"

"Do you think it would be proper?" Paul said.

"If you ask if something is proper one more time," she said with mock severity, "I'll scream. Remember this. I am the queen and whatever I do is proper. Anyway, I think it would be wonderful and cool."

Without second thoughts, the three men removed their heavy leather boots and their stockings. Dressed just in their tight uniform pants, they walked down toward the stream.

"I'll be there in a moment," Gloria said.

Quickly, she removed her heavy gown and her three petticoats. Dressed just in her camisole and pantaloons, Gloria walked down to the stream. The neckline of the camisole was low and the front was held together by three light blue ribbons. Her outfit left little to the imagination.

When the men saw her, they gasped. Her full breasts were clearly outlined and the dark brown nipples showed plainly.

"Let's wade in the cool water," Gloria said, laughing as she enjoyed the way the three men looked at her. She squealed as her feet touched the icy water, but she waded out into the middle of the stream by gingerly stepping on the mossy rocks.

"The rocks feel so soft and smooth under my feet," she said. "I love to stroke the soles of my feet on their fuzzy surfaces."

The three men didn't move. They continued to watch her every move, unable to take their eyes off her.

Queen Gloria put her foot on a round stone and then deliberately slid it off the far side. With a splash, she tumbled into the water. The three men ran to her rescue, slipping and sliding across the mossy stones. By the time they reached her, the front of her camisole was soaked, as were her white cotton pantaloons. The fabric clung to her small breasts and her mound was clearly visible. Each of the men reached out to help her up.

Gloria reached out to take the closest hand and gazed at the bulges, clearly visible through the men's tight, wet pants.

She pulled herself up and leaned against Mark's chest, her breasts pressing against him. She tipped her head back and gazed into his eyes. "Thank you for saving me," she whispered. Then she pressed her lips against his mouth until he couldn't help but respond. He wrapped his arms around her and kissed her deeply.

"Let's sit on the bank," she suggested as she pulled away. "You three must take off those pants. You're all soaked and must dry before we leave here."

When they reached the bank, Gloria reached out and pulled the front of Paul's pants open. He blushed as his erect penis sprang forth.

"You shouldn't be embarrassed. Your body is very beautiful." Gloria wrapped her hand around his engorged cock. "A very beautiful body," she murmured.

She turned and helped Tom remove his pants while Mark pulled his own off. "I'll have to help all of you get dry," Gloria said with a large grin.

"But, my lady," Tom said.

Gloria silenced him. "I am your queen and it is your duty to serve me. Right now, we all know how you can best serve me."

"Yes, Gloria," the three said.

Gloria knelt down on the grass and took Paul's large cock in her mouth. It was cool from the cold water and tasted particularly good in her hot mouth. Gloria looked up at his face. His eyes were closed and his mouth was open. His breathing was rapid and she knew he was ready to come. She was no novice at this form of entertainment and she loved how quickly the sensations she created drove Paul to the brink of orgasm.

As she felt Paul's muscles tense, she pulled back and flicked her tongue over the tip of his stiff penis. She wrapped her index finger and thumb tightly around the base of Paul's engorged cock to keep him from coming too quickly.

She turned to Mark, who stood and silently watched what she did. He was already partly erect, but as Gloria wrapped her hand around Mark's penis, it grew hard in her hand and moved as though it had a life of its own.

"How smooth your skin is," she said. "How big and hungry."

"Oh yes" was all he managed to say.

She lay back on the soft grass and spread her white thighs. She looked into Mark's eyes and smiled. "You know what I want you to do, don't you?"

Mark lost no time. He lay down between Queen Gloria's long legs and licked at her pussy. It was inflamed and wet and Mark licked up her salty juices.

"Kneel down," she said to the other two. One knelt on each side of her while Mark continued lapping at her cunt. She felt the tip of his tongue tickle her clit as her left hand found Tom's cock and her right found Paul's. She pulled and squeezed at the two penises, one short and thick, one long and slender. She reached underneath their bodies and stroked their balls.

Mark was driving her mad with his tongue, lapping and sucking like an expert.

"We mustn't fuck," Queen Gloria said hoarsely. "The king might find out."

"I think we can enjoy ourselves without fucking," Paul said as he tried to hold back his climax.

Mark was teasing her, forcing her closer and closer to orgasm. "I want you two to come with me," Gloria said. She threw her head back and tried to concentrate on her hands and Mark's tongue, all at the same time. She felt the heat boil in her belly and flow into her cunt and thighs.

"Right now!" she screamed as the tension burst and she came.

As she said *now,* Tom and Paul let loose their spurts of come, gobs of thick cream falling on Gloria's arms and chest.

After a few minutes, Mark crawled up beside Gloria and used a soft napkin to clean her off gently.

"It's your turn," she said to Mark when he was through.

Queen Gloria got on her knees and took Mark's cock in her mouth. Skillfully, she licked and sucked. She took her hand and stroked his balls until he was more excited than he had ever been.

Gloria pulled him out of her mouth just long enough to say, "Come in my mouth. I want to swallow every drop."

She wrapped her lips tightly around the base of his cock. Then, her lips still tight, she pulled back and sucked him in. It was like the tightest pussy he had ever felt. He came, spurting down her throat, and she swallowed every drop.

From then on, Queen Gloria and her servants made the trip to her parents' castle often. Everyone in the kingdom marveled at the loyalty of her entourage.

Eventually, the king died. Everyone in the kingdom expected the dowager queen to wed quickly, but she surprised everyone by remaining unmarried. However, she never lacked for sexual gratification, not with so many handsome uniformed men pledged to serve her in whatever way she wanted.

○ ● ○

THE SULTAN

Once upon a time, there was a sultan named Jamid. He was the undisputed ruler of a large kingdom that stretched into the desert in every direction as far as the eye could see.

The sultan was a man of thirty-five with straight almost-black hair and eyes that were so dark that the pupils couldn't be distinguished from the irises. His face and body were tanned to a dark chocolate brown. Fine straight hair covered his chest and arms.

When he sat on his throne, as he did now, he was the absolute master of everyone in the kingdom. He could order great riches or death with a wave of his hand.

He glared down at his grand vizier and tapped his restless fingers. "What are you bothering me with now?"

"The emissary from Persia is here, Your Majesty, and he says he has brought gifts."

The sultan merely nodded and the vizier scurried off to escort the emissary into the sultan's presence.

Moments later, the emissary entered and bowed low.

The sultan lounged on his throne, dressed in a blue and silver robe with full blue trousers and black boots underneath. He waved his hand and the emissary rose. "Yes, yes," the sultan said. "Get on with it."

"Your Highness," the emissary said, "I have brought you tribute from Persia, wondrous things to delight you." He clapped his hands twice.

Four slaves walked slowly into the room and each carried a large reed basket. The emissary spread an intricately woven Persian rug at the feet of the sultan. One at a time, three of the slaves opened their baskets and poured precious stones onto the carpet. Soon there was a large heap of diamonds, emeralds, and rubies, along with peridots, opals, and crystals of every color and shape.

The fourth slave bowed at the feet of the emissary and opened his basket. The emissary, like a magician, withdrew lengths of silk of every color and swirled them onto the floor over the jewels.

"That's nice," the sultan said. "Thank the King of Persia for me."

"But that's not all," the emissary said. "I have one more gift for you, more precious far than all these." He waved his hand over the jewels, then clapped three times.

The four slaves left the room and returned holding a curtain made of bloodred silk, woven with silver threads. They walked toward the throne and when they got near the sultan, they swept the curtain aside to reveal a tiny figure covered with silken veils of every hue.

"For your pleasure, Your Highness," the emissary said.

One by one, he began to remove the veils, until the tiny figure was covered, head to foot, only in a veil of pure spun silver.

"You may want to have the rest of your court leave, Your Highness, so only your eyes will behold the beauty I have brought you," the emissary said.

The sultan made a tiny nod and the vizier herded everyone out of the throne room. When the sultan, the vizier, and the emissary were alone with the tiny figure, the emissary dramatically removed the silver veil. The lower half of the virgin's face was covered with a tiny veil of pure gold, but otherwise she was naked.

The sultan sat up and looked her over carefully. Her skin was a flawless light beige that had never seen the light of the sun. Her breasts were small, ripe globes of tempting flesh. Her hips were narrow and her legs were long and magnificently shaped. Between her legs, her hair had been shaved to reveal her pouting lips.

She stood absolutely still except for her hands, which trembled at her sides.

"I want to see her face," the sultan said as his eyes roamed the virgin's body.

The virgin's head had been respectfully lowered, so the emissary raised her face to the sultan. Then, in one swift motion, he removed the last veil. The woman's eyes were downcast, but the sultan could see that they were blue, a very unusual color in his country. Her hair was golden and fell in long waves down her back. Her face was as beautiful as her body.

"Look at me," the sultan said.

The woman's eyes remained focused on the floor.

"She has never known any home but the woman's quarters of the palace in Persia, Your Highness," the emissary explained. "We have brought her here for you innocent. She was prepared for your entry by a eunuch several years ago, but she has never been taught the arts of love. We thought that you might enjoy teaching her yourself."

"What is your name?" the sultan asked.

"My name is Serena, Highness," she said, her voice barely audible.

"Do you want to serve me?" the sultan asked.

"Oh yes, Your Highness."

"Are you afraid of me?"

She hesitated, then decided to tell him the truth. "Yes, Your Highness."

The sultan roared with laughter. "At least you're honest. Look at me!" he commanded.

Serena raised her eyes and looked at the sultan for the first time. There was both fear and excitement in her gaze.

The sultan smiled. It would be a great pleasure to show her his power and then teach her about love.

"She is pure?" the sultan asked.

"Yes, Your Highness. She is completely innocent in the ways of love. I hope she pleases you."

"She will." The sultan turned to his vizier. "Take her to the woman's quarters and prepare her. Then bring her to me tonight."

"Yes, Your Highness."

That evening, Serena was brought to the sultan's rooms naked. She was surprised that she and the sultan were not alone. Four male slaves stood next to the sultan, and across the room two girls looked at her and whispered. Everyone was as naked as she was.

The slave who had brought her pushed her into the room and closed the door behind her. She bowed low and remained there, not knowing what she was supposed to do.

"Come here, Serena," the sultan said.

Barefoot, she padded to the sultan's chair. She wanted to cover her bare breasts but didn't dare.

"Do you know what goes on between a man and a woman?" he asked.

Her reply was a blush that covered her entire body.

The sultan snapped his fingers. Two slaves came forward and, with little ceremony, removed all his robes.

"Look at me," the sultan said. "Have you ever seen a naked man before?"

Again, she was silent.

He held his limp penis. "This is what I will use to open your love portal. I will show you how it is done."

Again, he snapped his fingers. "Anita, come here."

A girl of twenty, about Serena's age, came forward. "I wish to show Serena how it is between a man and a woman," he said. "Make me ready."

Anita got down on her knees and drew the sultan's penis into her mouth. She sucked it deeply, then slowly pulled away and let her lips hold it tightly. She repeated her in-and-out movements until the sultan's cock was fully erect.

Serena shook as she stared at his huge erection. That cannot possibly fit into my body, she thought.

"Show me what you have learned so far," the sultan said. "Suck on it yourself."

Serena hesitated.

"You must learn that when I tell you to do something, you do it. Without question. Do you understand?"

Serena nodded.

"I will let it pass this time. Should you hesitate again, I will have to show you my displeasure."

Serena knelt before the sultan and looked at his cock.

"Touch it," he said, "and put it into your mouth as you saw Anita do."

She touched it with her fingers and wrapped her hand around its girth. She wanted to please him but she was terrified. She shuddered, pulled back, and looked up at the sultan.

He said nothing, but instead looked at one of his slaves. Serena followed his gaze. The slave held a whip, which Serena was sure he wouldn't hesitate to use if the sultan ordered him to.

"You understand. Now, do as you're told."

She held him again, licked her lips, and touched her mouth to the tip of his erect cock. She felt him shiver as she took him deep into her throat. Then she pulled her head back but kept a vacuum in her mouth as she withdrew. After a few strokes, he grasped the back of her hair and pulled her face away.

"You learn quickly," he said. He pulled her upright, reached down, and poked a finger into the naked folds between her legs. She was still dry, but the sultan wasn't surprised. He had lots of patience and this girl would be worth the wait and the trouble of training her.

"Let me show you how fucking is done. Anita," he called, "present yourself to me for fucking."

Anita stretched out on the bed, her legs spread wide. She touched her mound to demonstrate that, unlike Serena, she was ready for him to enter her.

Serena tried to look away but felt the sultan's hand wind in her hair. He gripped her tightly and held her head so it faced the bed. "You must watch how this is done so you may learn."

The sultan bent over Anita's body and began to suck on her nipples. Gradually, as Anita became more and more excited, the sultan's licking moved lower, until his tongue was firmly lodged between her legs. As Serena watched, he licked, pressing his tongue deeply into all the folds of Anita's flesh.

The sultan looked at Serena. "I wish to save my cock for you, my dear," he said, "but there are ways to give pleasure without using my penis." He turned back and worked his tongue over Anita's swollen clit.

Serena wanted to look away but she was also fascinated, so she continued to watch.

The sultan's tongue licked and flicked as he reached up and squeezed Anita's nipples. He changed his cadence, first licking with quick strokes, then slow, long passes of his tongue. Suddenly, he plunged his tongue deep into Anita's body. She screamed and climaxed.

The sultan stood up and looked at Serena. "Do you see what pleasure a woman can get?"

"Yes, Your Highness."

"Would you like me to love you like that? It would please me if you wanted it, but it is no real matter. I will have you one way or the other."

Serena took a deep breath and let it out slowly. She was surprised as she realized that she did want it. "I want to please you, Highness," Serena whispered.

"Then arrange yourself on the bed."

Serena stretched out on the bed. She already felt a tingling sensation between her legs and her juices made her slippery as she moved.

The sultan leaned down and tasted her wetness. "You are already ready for me," he said, smiling, "but I want to show you some of the joys that are in store for someone who learns to please and take pleasure."

He used his long fingers to hold her lips wide
open and, first gently, then firmly, he licked and
tasted her. As he felt her get more and more
excited, he reached up and took one of Serena's
erect nipples in his fingers. Serena gasped as the
sultan flicked her tight bud with the tip of his
tongue and nipped it with his teeth while he
pinched and squeezed her tender nipples. She
thrashed her head back and forth as her body
became more and more excited. Soon, Serena
could stand no more. With the sultan's tongue
inside of her, she climaxed, screaming.

Quickly, the sultan lay down on the bed and
pulled Serena on top of him. He raised her to a
sitting position, then lifted her hips and impaled
her slippery body on his erection.

"I like to see your beautiful breasts right above
my face." He took one nipple in his fingers and
pulled her over so that her breasts hung over his
mouth. He lifted his head and took one in his
mouth and suckled.

He sucked and pumped upward until his penis
erupted.

Moments later, the sultan lay back on the bed,
satisfied.

"You learn well," the sultan said. "Now you can
retire for the night and rest up for tomorrow's
lesson. There are many more things to learn."

○ ● ○

MIRROR, MIRROR

Once upon a time, there was a princess in a tiny kingdom. Princess Veronica had long golden hair and a heart-shaped face with blue eyes and soft pink cheeks. Her lips were small but promised a sensual kiss for any man who would dare to kiss her, but no one ever had kissed the princess. She was her father's oldest child and, as such, she was heir to the throne. Therefore, from her birth, no one had been allowed anywhere near her except her mother—the queen—and an array of nurses, governesses, and tutors.

On the day of her eighteenth birthday, Veronica's father threw a lavish party for her. He invited everyone of importance in his realm and handsome princes from every one of the adjoining kingdoms. It was time to choose a husband for the princess.

Huge tables were set up in the great hall of the castle to accommodate the hundreds of guests. A sumptuous feast was served and everyone ate heartily. During the meal, the king carefully pointed out each of the princes and extolled his virtues. It mattered very little to him which of the eligible men she chose, as long as she chose one quickly and started making little princesses and princes of her own. The princess studied each of the princes and tried to imagine what it would be like to spend her life with one of them. She knew that her father wanted only her happiness and would listen carefully to her wishes.

After dinner, the dancing began and Princess Veronica danced with each of the suitors. She talked with each of them and tried to imagine joining her life with his and jointly ruling the large kingdom.

"They're all so dull," she quietly told her mother. "One is more boring than the last. The idea of being closed up in this castle with any one of them makes me miserable. They treat me like some delicate flower, incapable of any feelings. I doubt that any one of them would even touch me, except maybe once a year when it was necessary to make another baby."

Her mother smiled indulgently, but she also realized that there was no escape from the need to make a decision that weekend.

After the dancing, gifts were presented to the princess. Her parents gave her a small château for her and her prince to live in after their marriage, before she became queen. Each of her sisters gave her a beautiful hand-embroidered gown covered with precious jewels. Dozens of wealthy landowners from throughout the land gave her gifts, as did each of the hopeful princes, one gift duller than the last. By the end of the evening, the princess had seventeen golden goblets with various precious stones, six diamond necklaces, and three new carriages, each with liveried drivers and footmen. It was all she could do not to yawn in everyone's faces.

Just when Veronica thought all the gift giving was finished, a short, motherly-looking woman bustled into the back of the hall. "I'm sorry I'm late," she said, puffing, "but my gift was late in arriving, and my coach broke a wheel. But here I am, darling Veronica, and it's time for my gift."

As the woman bustled down the center aisle of the great hall, Veronica heard a gasp. "It's Queen Bella of Maravia," someone said.

Queen Bella was Veronica's godmother but, because of the war between the two countries, she hadn't seen her goddaughter since Veronica's fifth birthday.

"What's that woman doing here?" the king muttered. "We've been at war with Maravia for more than ten years. I'll have her thrown out."

"Hush," the queen said under her breath. "She's Veronica's godmother and the trouble between our kingdom and hers occurred when Veronica was just a small girl. They exchange letters and so Veronica is very fond of her. I won't have you making a scene at this party."

The king relaxed a bit. "As long as she's not here to make trouble."

Veronica smiled broadly. "Godmother," she said, "I'm glad you came."

"Yes, yes, dear," her godmother said, "it's good to see you, too, in spite of your father." Queen

Bella glared at the king. "And you're so grown-up and so beautiful. Let me give you my gift so you can use it this very night."

The godmother clapped her hands. Four footmen marched dramatically down the center of the great hall, carrying a large, flat, square package.

With great ceremony, Veronica's godmother unwrapped the gift and revealed a large gilt mirror.

"Hang this mirror on your wall tonight and gaze into it," her godmother said. "It is said that if a princess stares very hard into this magic mirror and says, 'Mirror, mirror on the wall, who's the most perfect man of all?' she will see the face of her prince charming."

Veronica didn't believe in magic but she loved her godmother and wouldn't hurt her feelings. She walked over to her godmother and kissed her on the cheek. "Thank you, Godmother," she said. "I will hang the mirror this very moment."

Veronica said a hasty farewell to the guests at the feast and hurried to her bedroom, followed by the four footmen. It took very little time for them to hang the mirror on the princess's wall.

When the task was completed, the footmen left and the king, the queen, and the princess's godmother entered.

The king was still muttering under his breath because Veronica's mother had made Queen Bella welcome despite his objections. She had even found a room for her for the night.

The king and queen bade their daughter good

night. "A mirror," the king mumbled as he and his wife left the room. "What kind of a gift is that?"

Her godmother kissed Veronica good night and started to leave. As she was about to close the door behind her, she turned and winked at the princess. "Use the mirror tonight and I am sure you will be well pleased."

Quietly, Queen Bella closed the door and left Veronica alone, standing before the mirror.

After a long hesitation, Veronica decided that she had nothing to lose. "Mirror, mirror on the wall," Veronica said, feeling very silly, "who's the most perfect man of all?"

She stared into the mirror and saw nothing but her own reflection.

"How foolish I am," she said aloud, "to believe a silly legend."

Sadly, she realized that she would have to marry one of the boring princes. Slowly, she removed her ball gown and slippers, her camisole and six petticoats. She carefully put her jewelry away in beautiful velvet boxes. Dressed only in her silk pantaloons, she stood in front of the mirror one last time and looked at herself. Her breasts were small and high, her nipples large and dark. Her waist was tiny and her stomach flat and smooth.

She reached up and touched her naked breasts. She watched her hands in the mirror as they slid over her smooth flesh. Slowly, she swirled her fingertips over the pale skin around her now-erect nipples.

She heard herself purr as her fingers pinched and pulled at her nipples, making them project from her chest, hard and hungry. Her hands began to stroke her flat belly and then they slowly slid down under the waistband of her pantaloons. Her eyes closed so she could savor the feelings.

"What a waste," a man's voice said from behind her.

Her eyes flew open. In the mirror, she saw the face of one of the footmen who had brought in the mirror. He had entered her bedroom silently while her eyes were closed and now was standing just behind her back. He was peering over her shoulder at her naked body.

The footman had straight dark hair and light gray eyes. His features were handsome and his body was tall and muscular.

"How d-d-dare you enter my room?" the princess stammered.

"I entered in your moment of need," the handsome footman said. "My name is Charles and I'm here to serve you."

He reached around and cupped one breast with each of his hands. He tickled her nipples with his fingers as he bent his head and pressed his warm lips against the nape of her neck.

"You mustn't do that," the princess protested. "I'm a princess and no one must touch me."

"I am touching you," he murmured into her neck, "and you are enjoying it."

Her knees felt weak and his tongue swirled over

the back of her neck and his hands teased and pinched her nipples.

"You must stop," she said weakly. Her head fell back and rested against the footman's chest.

"Open your eyes," he said softly, "and watch what I'm doing. I want you to see everything."

Veronica opened her eyes. His long fingers were pulling at her breasts and she found that watching did enhance the pleasure.

Her arms hung limply at her sides, but her palms ached to feel the footman's flesh beneath them. Slowly, the man's hands began to inch down her body. His palm stroked her flat belly as hers had done only minutes before.

When his fingers reached the silken bow that held the top of her pantaloons, he pulled one of the ends. The bow untied easily and the silken material soon lay in a heap around her feet.

"Watch in the mirror, Princess, as I give you pleasure."

His fingers began to probe her mound, threading their way through her silky hair toward her wet, open center. Her body sagged against him, but she continued to watch him pleasure her.

Charles backed up until the backs of his legs were against the bed. Still reflected in the mirror, he sat down and pulled Veronica onto his lap, with her back against his chest. He spread her legs and held them apart with his knees.

Veronica had never seen herself this way before, her pussy wide open, with the footman's fingers playing with the folds of her flesh. She could feel his hardness pressing against her lower back. As she moved her hips in rhythm with his fingers, her buttocks rubbed against his erection.

Despite his rising passion, he continued to play with the princess's wet cunt. His fingers slid partway into her but then pulled out before she felt any satisfaction. Again and again, he teased her as he alternated between her opening and her clit, swirling his fingers through her moisture.

Her eyes never left the mirror as she soared higher and higher. She placed her tiny pale hands over the footman's large bronze ones as they stroked her body. The footman recognized her need and, with her hands on his, he inserted first one, then two, and finally three fingers deep into her. He pounded in and out while his other hand stroked her clit.

As she watched her hands and his giving her pleasure, she felt a tightening in her belly. What's happening to me? she wondered. It's so beautiful and so terrible. This heat inside of me will never stop.

Higher and higher she climbed until, suddenly, she climaxed. The footman felt her body contract against his fingers. Waves of pleasure flowed over her and her juices filled his hands.

When her body subsided, he stood and undressed. As she watched him, he said, "I would like to make love to you but I cannot, not yet. Would you give me pleasure like I gave it to you?"

She smiled and nodded. He took her hand,

wrapped it around his cock, and showed her how to stroke him and fondle his balls. It took only moments until his semen spurted into her palm.

He lay down on the bed next to her and they both fell into a light sleep.

Later, they talked together. "You must leave," she said. "No one must know about this."

"Wouldn't you like me to stay?" the footman asked.

"More than anything," she said. "But I'm a princess and you will be killed if anyone finds you here."

"Who would do such a thing?" The footman chuckled.

"Stop taking this so lightly!" she snapped. "It's serious. Tomorrow the king will announce who my husband will be, and if he knows about you, he will have to kill you." She turned her face to his and kissed him. "It would kill me if anything happened to you."

"Then why don't you marry me?" the footman replied. "Didn't the legend say that you would see the face of your husband in the mirror?"

"It did, but you are just a footman and I must marry one of those dull princes whom my father invited to meet me."

The footman's smile broadened. "My mother thought you might decide that all of the princes were equally dull. She also knew that the king would have to obey your wishes, even if you chose a prince who hadn't been invited. She decided to sneak me in spite of the fact that your father refused to invite me."

Veronica propped herself upon her elbow. "I don't have any idea what you're talking about."

"I am Prince Charles of Maravia. My mother, your godmother, was sure that we would be perfect together, and now I agree with her. She has been trying to end the war between our two countries for many years, but your father wouldn't listen. She decided on this ruse to get us together in spite of your father's feelings. It will solve so many problems."

"Then you're a real prince?" Veronica asked.

"Crown and all," Charles said.

Veronica laughed and wrapped her arms around Charles's neck. "That's the best news I've had. And the mirror worked. It did show me the face of my future husband."

"It certainly did," the prince said. Then he rolled Veronica over and made love with her all night.

JACK AND JILL

Once upon a time, there was a young couple named Jack and Jill.

Jack and Jill enjoyed their occasional trips to a

spring about halfway up Hickory Mountain, where they would fill up several plastic containers with the fresh icy cold spring water that ran out of a fissure in the rock. The spring was in a remote area where few others ever visited, so sometimes they paused in their water-gathering efforts to make love in the open air. Today Jack had more elaborate plans.

They hiked up to the spring and enjoyed some time in the sun, sunbathing their favorite way— nude. After an hour or so, they devoured the magnificent lunch that they had brought along. After lunch, Jack filled several of the large plastic gallon jugs with water. By the time he finished, Jill was lying among the trees, taking a nap. Jack gazed down at Jill's sleeping face, then unzipped his knapsack and withdrew four long, soft ropes. Silently, he tied the ropes to four of the trees that surrounded Jill. As gently as he could, he tied each of Jill's wrists to one of the trees.

As she awakened, Jill was aware of Jack tying a rope to one of her ankles.

"Jack, what are you doing?" she asked.

"I'm getting ready to have some fun. As you can see, you're almost completely helpless, tied hand and foot and so beautiful."

"Jack, don't be ridiculous," she said. She had never been in such a situation before and she felt she should protest loudly. "Untie me this instant," she said, knowing what he had in mind. Being tied and helpless was making her very wet between her legs.

Jack finished tying one of her ankles. Then he reached up and ran his finger through the furry patch between Jill's legs. "You tell me to untie you, but you're soaking wet. Soon you'll see that you have no choice and you'll have to lie back and enjoy it."

He took Jill's other ankle and tied it to the fourth rope. When he was finished, he stood up and looked down.

"It excites me to see you so wide open for me. I love feeling that I can do anything I want to your luscious body."

Jill did indeed have a beautiful body. Her breasts were full and round, pulled up by the stretching of her arms over her head. Her bush was blond and matched her short blond hair. Her large moss-green eyes just looked at Jack and her tiny pink tongue licked her full red lips.

"You can't mean this, Jack," she said, hoping that he did mean all of it.

Jack said nothing as he walked over to the water jugs. Jill loved watching him walk. His ass was small and tight, below his broad shoulders and massive back. His arms and legs were well muscled from the many outdoor activities he enjoyed. His brown hair was shoulder-length and had a few sun-bleached blond streaks.

Jill couldn't remember ever being so excited. Jack returned with one of the plastic water jugs and a small nail. He took another rope and suspended the water jug between two branches so it hung over Jill's naked body. Then he used the nail to poke a small hole in the plastic.

He adjusted the bottle until a tiny stream of icy water began to fall on Jill's right nipple. Jack walked around to her left side and took her left nipple in his mouth. It was already hard from the effect of the cold water. He sucked while the cold water dripped on Jill's other breast. The combination of cold and warmth was driving Jill crazy.

Jack leaned forward and caught the stream in his mouth. He filled his mouth with icy water and then wrapped his lips around Jill's nipple. Icy water caressed her hot, swollen breast.

"Jack," she said, "you're driving me crazy. Untie me and then we can make love."

"Not yet, darling. Not for quite a while. I have a few more surprises for you."

"But I want you now," she begged.

Jack looked at her and smiled. "From what I see," he said, looking at the ropes that held her spread-eagled, "you have very little choice."

He stood up and momentarily stopped the stream of water. Jill sighed, glad that Jack was done playing.

Suddenly, she felt the stream, this time on her cunt. The water was dripping on her clit and trickling down between her legs. She started to move her hips, trying to move the stream of water away from her hot core. As her hips moved, the stream of water played across her wet lips and the ticklish places inside her thighs. It was sweet torture.

"I love to watch your hips writhe like that," Jack said.

Jill realized that moving just accentuated the teasing sensations. She was so hungry, but the frigid water was preventing her from climaxing. She pressed her hips into the ground and tried to hold still.

"That's a good girl," Jack said. "Just lie still while I get something else for us to play with."

Jill wondered what Jack was doing, but she couldn't concentrate. All she could think about was the stream of water between her legs.

Jack returned and spent a moment sucking her swollen breasts. Then he held something up for Jill to see. "What's that?" Jill said.

"I would think it was obvious, but I'll explain it, anyway. This," he said as he showed her the toy in his hand, "is a dildo. But it's a special kind. You're supposed to fill it with warm water so it feels more natural inside. In this case, however, it will feel a little different."

Jack reached up and took down the jug. Jill sighed, enjoying the cessation of the cold stream.

Jack began to lick Jill's frozen cunt. His tongue lapped at her flesh, stroking her from anus to clit. He could feel how hot Jill was and he didn't want her to climax too quickly. He picked up the dildo and touched Jill's hot pussy.

Jill screamed. "Jack, that's ice-cold."

Jack smiled. "I know. It should cool you off just a bit." He inserted the cold plastic into Jill's cunt and pushed the frosty dildo deeper inside. She thrashed and Jack wasn't sure whether she was trying to push the dildo out or suck it in.

Jack watched Jill's head whip from side to side as her hips bucked and her arms and legs strained against the ropes holding her open for him.

When the dildo was all the way into Jill's cunt, he started to lick her clit again.

The combination of hot and cold sensations was too much for Jill. She climaxed more violently than she had ever imagined possible.

She spasmed for a long time, then Jack pulled the dildo out and lay down beside her. They slept for a while. Then Jill was awakened to the feeling of Jack's fully erect cock pressing between her legs. Slowly, he pushed the entire length of himself into her, then he was still.

She felt a sudden cold on her clit. Jack was stroking her with the dildo, now full of icy fresh water. As he stroked and her hips moved, his erection pounded inside her.

She climaxed quickly and the spasms of her body pulled Jack's climax from him. Later, Jack untied Jill and they walked back down the hill.

From then on, they went up the mountain almost every week. And they lived happily ever after.

13
STORY STARTERS

Now that your imagination is working overtime, you may want to write your own story. My partner recently wrote one that combined many of his favorite fantasies, a story that was unlike anything I had written. We spent a few wonderful evenings with it. First, we spent an evening enjoying the sexual excitement that he had built up writing it, then on another evening I read it aloud to him. We spent other nights play-acting sections.

Some of you will be sufficiently relaxed to write your own story, but it's often very difficult to begin. It is embarrassing and very awkward to put your innermost sexual fantasies on paper, and even worse to show the results to your partner. But if you can, do it by all means. And don't worry about grammar or syntax, just write it. I can tell you from personal experience that it's fantastic.

To make creating your own fantasy a bit easier, here's a simpler way to put your imagination to use. This chapter contains a number of what I call story starters. Each short-story introduction consists of a scene and some characters who get themselves into a sexual situation. The story ends just as things are heating up.

Take some time and read through them, then suggest that your partner do the same. Find one that seems as if it would be fun to read aloud. Then, when my writing stops, improvise. What do the characters do? What do they say? You and your partner can continue the action and create alternate paragraphs. When you decide to stop talking and do something, that's when the real fun starts.

With all the stories that I have included in this and other sections of this book, I still may have missed your favorite fantasy. This is where you can associate freely and wander into your personal world. You can even write the rest of the story out, bookmark it, and give it to your partner.

Would you like to spank your partner or use a vibrator? How about showering together and making love under the running water? Maybe you'd like to take Polaroid pictures of your partner during lovemaking. There are as many sexual fantasies as there are people who fantasize.

If your partner is doing the improvisation, realize that he may be trying to suggest something in one of these fantasies. Be aware that maybe the time has come to go from talking to doing. Seize the moment.

○ ● ○

SEDUCTION

It had been almost three weeks since Herb had first read the article that his wife, Betty, bookmarked for him. She wanted to play seduction. She wanted to be seduced by a strange man on their first date.

At first, he had been insulted. The romance was certainly not gone from their thirty-year marriage. Was it? The more he thought about it, the more he realized that a little seduction wouldn't be out of place. It would be nice to recapture some of the old feelings.

Once he came to terms with the idea of seducing his wife, he spent many hours setting the scene and deciding on all the props he would need. If he was going to do it at all, he was going to do it right. He found that just fantasizing about slowly seducing his wife was unexpectedly exciting.

He was finally ready on a Thursday morning. First, he sent his wife a dozen yellow roses with a card saying, "Please have dinner with me this evening at a little Italian restaurant I know of. If it's all right with you, I'll pick you up at 6:30." He signed the note H. He thought about adding the word *Love*, but it didn't seem to go with the idea of seduction by a stranger.

Early in the afternoon, he found a telephone message on his desk: "Six thirty would be wonderful," and it was signed B.

Mid-afternoon, he went to a local men's store to look for a new image for the evening. Betty always commented that blue brought out the color of his eyes, so he selected a new dress shirt in a color between robin's egg and sky blue. While he was there, he bought a new dark blue striped tie. It was far from his usual style, and as he looked in the mirror at the picture he presented, he was pleased.

At exactly 6:30, he arrived at his own front door and rang the bell. Betty opened the door and didn't seem at all surprised that he hadn't used his key. She looked beautiful in a soft gray wool skirt and a silky pink blouse.

"You're right on time," she said. "I like that in a man."

They dined at a little Italian restaurant that had been recommended to him by a man in his office. He was delighted, more by the atmosphere than the fine food. The lights were low, with most of the illumination from candles on each table. There was soft violin music and there were little screens to separate each table from the others. Herb ordered a bottle of Chianti, which complemented the dinner.

During the meal, he and Betty made small talk. Both of them deliberately stayed away from the topics they usually discussed—the children, their friends, their hard days at work.

At one end of the room, there was a small dance floor. After the main course, they danced but held each other at a discreet distance. It was not yet time for intimacy.

On the way home, Betty asked, "Would you like to come in for a cup of coffee?"

It didn't seem at all silly that he was being invited to have coffee in his own house. "I'd like that," he said softly.

When they arrived home, Betty went into the kitchen to make coffee. Herb took advantage of the moment to take off his jacket and arrange a dozen candles around the living room. He turned off all the other lights and put some soft music on the phonograph.

Betty walked into the living room and Herb took the coffee from her. "Dance with me," he said in a husky voice.

They came together, their arms around each other. They held each other close and each felt the length of the other's body. Herb pressed his cheek against Betty's hair and inhaled her perfume. "I love your fragrance," he murmured in her ear.

"Thank you," she said. "Is this a new shirt?"

"I hoped you would like it," he said. It was suddenly very important that she liked his selection.

"It's extremely becoming."

As they swayed gracefully with the music, Herb sensuously caressed his wife's back from her neck to her waist. Suggestively, he pressed his erection against her belly and he felt her body respond. He breathed warm air on her ear and kissed her hair. The music ended, but he held her until the next song played. He was in no hurry.

They danced for half an hour and punctuated the music with long, luxurious kisses. Then he whispered in her ear, "Shall we go upstairs?"

She nodded. He kept his arm around her waist as they walked upstairs to the bedroom.

SUBMISSION

Suzanne had no idea what the stranger wanted, but she told James to put him in the front parlor while she freshened up in her room. What could he want with me? she wondered as she looked at herself in the glass. The face that looked back at her was more youthful than her twenty years would have indicated. Her large eyes were the color of deep blue water and her lips were soft and sensuously full. Her blond hair was fashioned into a pile of curls on top of her head and her full-skirted light rose morning gown enhanced her recently matured figure.

Well, she thought, there's nothing to do but ask him. She pinched her cheeks to enhance their natural color and left her room.

She glided gracefully down the central staircase

and opened the large oak door to the front parlor. Bright morning sunshine streamed through the tall casement windows and a shaft fell on the stranger as he stood next to Suzanne's father's desk.

As his back was to her, she took a minute to look at him. He stood with a lazy posture, his hand gracefully resting on the surface of the desk. His tight buff-colored breeches clung to his muscular thighs. His tightly fitted forest-brown jacket accented his broad shoulders. He turned and she gazed into a pair of deep brown eyes. He's a good-looking man, she thought as she approached him.

"Ah, Miss Armstrong," he said. His voice was soft and smooth, but Suzanne sensed a purpose beneath the casual tone.

"You obviously know me, sir, but have we met?"

"Not formally. I am Jeffery St. Marks, at your service." He inclined his head slightly.

"What can I do for you, Mr. St. Marks?"

"That's a bit of a long story. Shall we sit?"

Suzanne settled gracefully in a wing chair by the fireplace. "May I offer you some refreshments?"

"It's a bit early." He lazily surveyed her body. Lovely. Just lovely. And with her superior family history, she would do nicely. She was going to be worth all his trouble. Indeed she was.

She stared at him quizzically. When he offered no information, she said, "What can I do for you?"

"You can do a lot, my dear. I intend, probably this

very week, to make love to you, and then, if you please me as I suspect you will, to marry you."

Suzanne was appalled. How dare he! "My dear sir," she said, her eyes flashing, "I don't know what has made you think that I would sit here and listen to this nonsense, but whatever it was, you were sadly misled."

She started to rise, but Jeffery leaned forward and placed a strong hand on her forearm, holding her firmly. "I wouldn't be too quick," he said, his voice still soft. "I think you should wait until you hear my story before you ruin your life, as well as those of your parents."

Suzanne glared at Jeffery but remained seated.

"Before I explain, perhaps you would answer one question for me."

Suzanne continued to sit in stony silence.

Jeffery smiled. "You're already twenty years old, well past the age that women usually marry. Why haven't you married? You're so beautiful, surely you've had dozens of proposals."

"I don't think it's any of your concern, but I'll answer, if only to get rid of you. I was engaged to Philippe Martineaux when I was sixteen. It was a love match, but two months before the marriage, he died of the fever. My father said that I should wait until I fall in love again, and I've not met anyone since as good and kind as Philippe."

"I suspected as much. Thank you for your honest answer. You're learning already that cooperation is best. Now, let me explain my presence here.

Are you aware of your father's penchant for cards?"

When Suzanne merely continued to glare, Jeffery continued. "No, I guess not. Well, your father loves a good game of poker, but, alas, his luck hasn't been very good lately. And to his further misfortune, he tends to bet more heavily when he's losing, probably to try to recoup his losses."

"What has this got to do with me?" she snapped.

"Patience, my dear. It will all be obvious soon. Let me digress for a moment. Do you remember the Sheridans' masked ball?"

"Of course. I still don't understand what all this has to do with me?" She tried to pull her hand away, but he held fast.

"We were not introduced, but I saw you there, flirting outrageously with several young men." He closed his eyes and the corners of his mouth turned up. "You were ravishing in that gold Grecian gown you wore." He opened his eyes and looked at her. "I suppose you also remember your walk in the garden with a certain overanxious suitor who kissed you. You allowed his hands to roam very familiarly over your delectable body."

Suzanne's blush was her only reply.

"Obviously, you remember that, too. I was watching, aching to be that young man. You are most delectable, Miss Armstrong. Your body absolutely enchants me and my fingers ache to touch you like that young man was doing. I need a wife and I need sons, so right then and there I decided

I would have you." He felt her try to pull away, but his grip was too strong for her. "Don't get up just when I'm approaching the good part."

She glared at him, but he felt her relax just a bit. "Good. Now, here's where good fortune fell into my hands. I was playing cards at a certain gaming establishment a few nights ago when I chanced to encounter your father. He had had a few too many brandies and had gotten into a high-stakes poker game. Needless to say, he lost."

He could see understanding begin to dawn on Suzanne. "You beat him?" she asked.

"I didn't do it personally, but I was watching. His last few bets were outrageously large, but, unfortunately, his bad luck held."

"No wonder he's been behaving so strangely," Suzanne said, remembering his recent bouts of temper and long silences.

"After he left, I bought his IOUs. It was really very simple. Now I hold the power to call in the debts and force your father to surrender this fine estate to me with much unpleasantness and publicity or . . ."

Almost afraid to hear it put into words but unable to stop herself, Suzanne said, "Or what?"

"Or you can be mine. I'm not speaking of marriage just yet. I want to sample the merchandise before I make a decision. But, perhaps . . ."

"You can't mean what you're saying."

A slow, lazy smile played over Jeffery's face as he looked at Suzanne. His eyes caressed the swells of her breasts as her bosom heaved. As his gaze dipped into the inviting valley between them, his grip on her wrist tightened.

"Oh but I do," he said at last. "Let me set it all out for you. You have three choices. First, you can refuse me. In that case, I will go immediately to your parents and announce my plans to take over this house. They will, of course, have a few weeks to move out. I'd really prefer not to have to do that. It would be so unpleasant for the three of you."

"Or . . . ?"

"You can come with me to my home, where we will spend a beautiful week or two, exploring our compatibility with your complete cooperation."

"You said I had three choices."

"You can go with me but resist and fail to please me, in which case it will ruin your reputation. I will keep you with me for an entire week. Then I will tell everyone where you have been and exactly what we have been doing. There won't be much future for you then.

"I think your only true choice is to do everything in your power to please me, and I think you can. In that case, we will marry and I will give you your father's IOUs as a wedding present. Then, you will give me sons. Between times, you will give me your beautiful body to do with as I please. Do I make myself clear?"

Suzanne thought briefly, but she couldn't find a way out. "I guess I have only one choice."

Jeffery released Suzanne's wrist. "Shall we seal our bargain, my dear?" he said. He leaned over and pressed his lips against hers. As he deepened his kiss, he reached down the bodice of her dress and squeezed her nipple. She wanted to withdraw, but she knew she could not.

"I'll come back to pick you up in two hours. That will give you time to pack a few things and discuss our arrangement with your parents. You may tell them whatever you wish about why you're going with me, but be ready when I return." He rose and bowed low. "Until then, my dear."

He took her hand and raised it to his lips, but instead of kissing the back, he turned it over and swirled his tongue in her palm.

She sighed and her shoulders slumped. "Until then," she said.

COMPULSION

More than a hundred years ago, there lived a doctor who had devoted the ten years following his graduation from medical school to the development of potions and gadgets that would drive women to the wildest heights of passion.

He lived in a large mansion near a small village where, periodically, a stranger, man or woman, would disappear. They would return weeks or months later healthy and happy, but with no recollection of anything that had transpired. If any of the villagers suspected what went on, no one ever spoke.

No one had ever actually seen the mansion, since the hedges around the property had long been encouraged to grow to enormous heights. No one had ever seen the doctor. The only one from the mansion who was seen in the village was Walter, the doctor's loyal servant. Once a week, on market day, he would go to the village to buy food.

One fateful day, Theresa, a beautiful girl from a faraway town, ran away from her wicked uncle. He had cared for her since her parents' death, when she was a baby, and until recently she had been resigned to her lot. For most of her nineteen years, he had forced her to work on their farm from sunup to sundown. He had dressed her in rags and kept her a virtual prisoner. Finally, early one morning, her uncle came into her room in the loft and found her undressed. He looked at her for a long time, then told her that he was going to marry her and keep her with him always. She had run away that afternoon.

For many days, she wandered the countryside, looking for a kind farmer or shopkeeper to take her in. She was a hard worker and had been sure that she could find employment, but it had been more than a week and still she had found no one willing to do more than let her spend a night in the barn before she moved on. Now, she was hungry and scared and not so sure that running away had been such a good idea.

She was wandering around the village square one market day when Walter spotted her. Despite her filthy appearance, he recognized immediately that she was a beautiful woman. It had been such a long time, he thought, and she will do nicely. His cock grew hard just watching her move from stall to stall.

He asked around about her family and soon learned the truth. No one would miss her. She was a perfect subject for the doctor.

"Young woman," Walter said, stepping beside her. "I understand you're looking for work."

"Why yes, sir," she said, smiling sweetly. "I'm a good worker. I could help in the kitchen or I could—"

"That's fine," Walter said, "you're hired. I'll take you to the house when I'm finished here. I just need to buy a few more things. Take this and follow me." He thrust the basket he was carrying into her hands and walked off before she could see the gleam in his eyes.

Theresa was delighted. It seemed that finally she had found work. She ignored the saddened stares of the people in the market square and trailed after Walter as he finished his shopping.

An hour later, as they approached the mansion, Theresa wondered whether she should have accepted this job. They had already passed through the huge iron gate, the only opening in the forbidding hedge, and Walter had locked it behind them.

With sure, quick steps, Walter led Theresa around to the kitchen entrance and introduced her to the cook. "Put her to work, Molly," he said brusquely. Then he turned and left the room.

A few minutes later, Walter met the doctor in his laboratory. "I have found a new subject for us. She appears to be eighteen or nineteen and she has long brown hair and wide-set brown eyes. With a bath and a few good meals, you'll realize that her shape is magnificent, her skin is like fine marble, and her lips are like rubies. She looks a little like that woman we had so much fun with a few years ago. Please, sir, can I have her when you're done?"

"What about her family?" the doctor asked, ignoring Walter's request.

"She has run away from her uncle, who lives many miles from here." Walter looked at his master, a tall, handsome man of thirty-seven with raven-black hair and flashing black eyes. Walter had spent years wondering how the doctor had started his experiments, but all he had ever learned was that it had something to do with a woman who had spurned his affections when he was a teenager. Walter didn't care how it started; he just enjoyed his part in them.

"Where did you put her?"

"She's in the kitchen helping the cook."

"Fine. See that she's bathed and fed. Then put the 'medicine' in her food, starting with a small dose tomorrow night. In a week, I'll decide exactly where to start with her."

For three days, Theresa worked quietly in the kitchen. She was kept very busy all day, so, after her dinner, she collapsed on her bed in the attic and slept soundly until she was awakened to start work the next morning.

On the night of the fourth day, she had strange dreams, which, although she could not remember them when she awoke, left her with a strange hunger that she couldn't quite understand.

All the fifth day, she was restless, unable to concentrate on her work. A strange longing possessed her and caused her to drift off into bizarre thoughts. The cook paid little attention. She had seen it before, starting when she, herself, had been in Theresa's situation.

That night, Theresa's dreams were more erotic and they made her nipples hard and created an itch or ache between her legs. When she awoke in the middle of the night, she pressed her hand between her thighs and tried to still the throbbing she felt. Then she ran her palms over her swollen nipples. She fell back to sleep with her fingers still pressing her hot flesh, and she remembered little the next morning.

The next night's dreams inflamed her senses, and the depth of the lingering sensations had increased. By noon, it was hard for her to sit still or keep her hands from straying to her groin. Her breasts were hot and sore and her constantly erect nipples itched where they pressed against the front of her simple kitchen dress.

It was in that state that Walter found her. "The doctor would like to meet you," he said.

Theresa followed Walter toward the doctor's

workroom, rubbing her thighs together as she walked to try to ease the sensations.

As she entered the room, she saw the doctor looking at her. "She'll do nicely," she heard him say. "Very nicely indeed."

CONTROL

Bonnie's surroundings faded in as she returned to consciousness. She had no concept of where she was or how she had gotten there.

The first of her senses to return was her hearing. She became aware of a dull, slow throb, so low in pitch that she wasn't sure whether she heard it or felt it—like huge engines, far away. And there was a faint medicinal smell.

Her eyes were closed, yet she knew that the room was light. Without moving the rest of her body, she ran one finger over the surface on which she was lying. It was hard, like metal or stone, but it was faintly warm, like some kind of heated plastic.

Over the sound of the throbbing engines, she sorted out the sound of breathing. Someone else was in the room with her. She risked opening her eyes just a crack, since she had learned all she could with her eyes closed. She peeked out through her long lashes.

The ceiling glowed. It wasn't lights behind a translucent substance; the ceiling glowed all on its own. The walls didn't look metal. They looked like soft blue plastic, maybe similar to the substance of the couch on which she was lying.

She opened her eyes all the way and looked around. She was not lying on a couch but, rather, on a table. On a parallel table lay the unconscious figure of a man, in a full dress suit.

She reasoned that she should be terrified, but she wasn't. It was as though she was enveloped in a blanket of calm.

"Where are we?" she said to the air. To her surprise, the air answered.

"You are here with us," the disembodied voice said. She was reminded of her father's voice when he calmed her after a nightmare.

"Where is that?"

"You wouldn't understand," the voice said gently.

"Who the hell are you?" the man on the other table said, his head turned toward her. She saw that he was strapped down to the table, and as she started to sit up, Bonnie realized that she, too, was restrained.

"Forgive the restraints," the voice explained. "We were afraid you might injure yourselves."

"My name is Bonnie," she said to the man on the other table, "Bonnie Walker. Who are you?"

"Neil," he said, glaring at her as if his being there was her fault. "Neil Harris."

"Now that you know each other's names," the voice said, "there are things we should tell you."

"Who we are is of no importance," a different voice continued. "Suffice it to say that we are from a place very far away and we have been sent here on a scientific mission."

"Is this some kind of joke?" Neil snapped. He glared at Bonnie.

"I assure you, Mr. Harris," she said, "I have no more idea of what's happening than you do."

"Don't be so upset, Mr. Harris," a second disembodied voice said. "I assure you that this is no joke. The more relaxed and accepting you are, the better, for both of you."

"We mean you no harm," the first voice said. "After we learn what we need to know, you will be returned and it will be as though nothing happened."

Bonnie's mind was whirling. Five minutes ago, she had been in her living room, recovering from an all-night party. Now she was here, wherever that was. She studied her cell mate. From what she could tell, he was a man about her age.

"Since you are calm now, we can dispense with the restraints," the voice said.

"How can you be so sure that we are calm?" Neil asked.

"Because we can feel what you are feeling." The second voice sounded as if it was instructing a small child.

There was a beep and the restraints disappeared. They didn't slide away or unfasten, they just disappeared. Both Bonnie and Neil sat up. While Bonnie remained sitting on the table, Neil got up and walked around the small room.

"No door," he muttered. "No openings or seams of any kind." He turned to Bonnie and sighed. "I'm sorry I seemed gruff before. I'm not used to coming home, collapsing on my sofa, and then resurfacing like this." He gestured at the room.

His smile seemed genuine as he admitted, "It's strange. I should be angry, or afraid. But instead I feel so calm, somehow."

"That is because we caused your fear to fade," the first voice said. "Fear serves no purpose. For what we have in mind, you need to be relaxed."

"Oh?" Neil said. "And what exactly is that?"

"We have surveyed all your literature and tried to understand you. We find we are at a loss to understand your sexual practices."

Bonnie chuckled. "Sometimes we don't understand them, either."

"It seems so complicated, unnecessarily so," the first voice said. "We simply build new models when we need them, which is seldom, since we seldom cease to exist."

"No sex?" Bonnie giggled. "How dull." Her sex life was anything but dull.

"So what do you want from us?" Neil asked.

"We selected two of your species, one male and one female. We selected you based on the fact that both of you are very sexually active and you seem to be able to find partners without much difficulty."

"My sexual partners are none of your business," Bonnie snapped.

Neil laughed warmly. "Come, come, Miss Walker, this is no time for modesty. They seem to know us well."

Bonnie turned away, excited but faintly embarrassed.

"We want to learn, and the only way we can learn," the second voice continued, "is by being inside your mind while you make love."

Neil raised his eyebrows. "You mean the same way you knew that we weren't afraid?"

"You understand us very quickly, Mr. Harris."

"This locale is hardly conducive to sexual activity," Neil said. "Usually sex is done in private, without anyone watching"—Neil paused—"or feeling."

"I know that you are no stranger to public displays. Surely you remember a certain Annabelle—"

"That's enough," Neil snapped.

Bonnie burst out laughing. "It seems we've been selected to be partners in a public display of our primitive sexual practices."

"What if we refuse," Neil said. "I, for one, don't make love on command."

"You can refuse to cooperate willingly, of course," the voice said, "but, if you do, we have many alternatives. We can force you to do whatever we want, or we can arrange to make you feel irresistible sexual hunger."

Neil and Bonnie thought about their predicament. Then they looked at each other and shrugged. He really is a very attractive man, Bonnie thought. She could feel a tingle of hunger grow deep in her belly. Bonnie didn't know whether her arousal was genuine or being placed there by the voices. She found she didn't care.

Neil was obviously having similar thoughts. His eyes studied her and his expression became openly sensual.

They felt or sensed the presence of the voices inside of their heads. "We wish to experience all the varieties we have read about in your publications. We will put different desires in your mind and remove all inhibitions."

Neil's eyes met Bonnie's.

"Shall we start with kissing?" the voices said.

ISOLATION

As the icy rain dribbled down the back of her neck, Trisha wondered why she had picked this afternoon to end up so far away from home.

Earlier that day, she and her aunt had quarreled— she didn't even remember what about—and she had stormed out of the house. She had walked for hours, getting farther and farther away from the farm. As the first cold drops fell from the leaden sky, she looked around and realized that she had no idea where she was.

"Damn," she said aloud as the rain got heavier. Her long hair lay in a flat, wet sheet down her back. Her soaked shirt and light jacket did little to protect her from the frigid drops.

Her teeth started to chatter and her fingers felt like icicles as she jammed them into her pockets. She spotted a huge tree and ran toward it, hoping to find some shelter from the deluge. The bolt of lightning that split the sky eliminated the tree as shelter.

She shivered violently, and tears started to form in her eyes. Not thunder, please, she prayed. Then she realized that she had to get out of the rain. I won't panic, she thought. There has to be somewhere I can go. There just has to be.

She looked across a small stream and, through the sheets of rain, she saw a tiny cabin nestled at the foot of a small hill. "Thank God," she whispered.

She ran across the little wooden bridge that led to the cabin and pounded on the door.

"Oh, please let me in!" she cried. "Please."

As she was almost ready to drop from exhaustion, she heard the bolt being pulled and then the door opened.

"Come in, come in. You're soaked." The man who opened the door was very tall, with sandy hair and large dark brown eyes.

"My name is Rick. I don't often get visitors," he said kindly. "I'm kind of a hermit out here, and I like it that way, but you're more than welcome."

Trisha walked in, introduced herself, and briefly explained how she happened to be there.

Rick looked at the puddle she was leaving on the floor. "You have to get out of those wet clothes." He rummaged through a small trunk that held his possessions. Trisha looked around the one-room cabin: a bed, a chair, a fireplace, and the trunk.

Rick held a pair of slacks and a man's shirt out to her. "These will have to do until we can dry your clothes."

He handed her a towel and showed her to the tiny bathroom. "We're not equipped for anyone but me, I'm afraid."

Ten minutes later, Trisha emerged from the bathroom. The shirt was tremendous and she had rolled the sleeves up to her elbows. She held the pants up with one hand and held her wet clothes in the other.

Rick took her clothes from her and grinned. "You don't look as much like a drowned rat, now," he said. "Come sit over here." He motioned to a spot on the rug in front of the fire and draped her clothes over the back of his only chair to dry.

Trisha settled on the soft rug and ran her fingers through her tangled long hair. "Do you have a comb?" she asked.

Rich pulled his comb out of his pocket with a flourish and handed it to her. "At your service," he said.

After a few frustrating moments pulling at the knots, she sighed.

"Can I help?" he asked. "I don't have a lot of experience combing a woman's hair, but it doesn't look too hard. And I'll bet it is easier for me than for you."

He meticulously started to work the knots out of her hair. As the fire dried it, it began to feel like a satin waterfall, long and straight and reaching almost to her waist.

There was a flash of lightning and a thunderous crash outside. Trisha jumped and a tiny sound escaped her lips.

"It's all right. The lightning can't hurt you." Under his fingers, Rick could feel Trisha shake.

"I've been afraid of lightning and thunder all my life," she whimpered. "I guess while I was trying to get dry, I shut out the storm. Now that I'm dry and comfortable, the lightning and thunder terrify me."

Gently, Rick took her in his arms. "I won't let anything hurt you. Just rest here with me and I'll take care of everything."

It felt so safe in his arms that Trisha cuddled deeper and looked up. She saw his lips descending on hers and she smiled. She wanted him to kiss her. She wanted to feel safe and protected in his arms.

The kiss was long and deep. When he pulled away, she knew that she didn't want him to stop.

She reached up and wrapped her hand around the back of his neck. She pulled his mouth down to hers. They both knew what they were saying. They knew that they wouldn't stop.

CONCLUSION

Variety is the spice of sexuality. Once you've found a game or a fantasy that you enjoy, don't think that you can use it every night for months. It will become stale. Anything becomes tiresome when overused. There is nothing inherently wrong with missionary position; it's just that it becomes routine.

Keep varying your sexual experiences. Try something new anytime it occurs to you. Reread the material in this book and mark a new story, one you've never played with before. Read more erotica, rent a videotape, try a new game.

A delicious warning. My partner has had a lot to do with this book. He's not only the inspiration, he's my primary editor. As you can imagine, we've read and reread this many times. Yesterday, he reread and edited this text and last night we tried something new, something again inspired by what he had read. There is no end to the variations. There are only the limits you place on yourself.

Have fun.

Dear Reader:

It would please me to know that you and your partner shared a wonderful experience that was in part due to my book.

I'd love to hear from you, so please write to me care of Warner Books, 666 Fifth Avenue, New York, NY 10103.

Thanks.